CW01584149

A.J. Ball

"GOD FELL OUT OF BED"

Grosvenor House
Publishing Limited

This book is published by
Grosvenor House Publishing Ltd
28-30 High Street, Guildford, Surrey, GU1 3EL.
www.grosvenorhousepublishing.co.uk

A CIP record for this book
is available from the British Library

ISBN 978-1-78148-018-2

To Esther

CONTENTS

Also by A.J.Ball

Books
The Closing of the Gate
A Spark of Time

Short stories

Magazine articles

Series
In and Around Bury
In and Around Selby
illustrated with my pen and ink sketches

Caricatures and cartoons

Sermons
Religious articles

Acknowledgements:
Bolton Evening News
The Bury Times
Methodist Recorder
Prediction
Sheffield Newspapers

All things work together
(intermingle) for good...
Romans 8, 28

PREFACE

Over the years, I wrote short stories and articles for newspapers and magazines, illustrating the articles with my pen-and-ink drawings. Mostly the stories were of events I experienced and people I met in World War II as an Army chaplain attached to a Casualty Clearing Station in the Far East. I had thought of collecting those published stories into book form. Then I decided to write my autobiography, covering the years from my birth 1913 to 1947, including a few of those stories. I have made each chapter as far as possible a separate story. Beginning as a child of five on 'Armistice Day 1918' (Chapter 1), including the end of the War 'VJ Day in Bombay' (Chapter 15) and concluding with 'Two Choices' (Chapter 33) in 1947. There are fictitious names for a few persons. A suggested title for the autobiography, "God fell out of bed" is a quotation from 'The Jewel Revealed' (Chapter 27). I have the written permission from editors of The Bolton Evening News, The Bury Times and Prediction to use the whole or parts of the work they published. My acknowledgements are due to them, also to Dr Mace for use of his typewritten record of a conversation "A Question of Conscience" (Chapter 16). I thank my son Chris for his computer wizardry with the illustrations.

Albert J Ball

1

CHILDHOOD & SCHOOL

Chapter 1

Armistice Day

Armistice Day, November 11, 1918; I was then a five-year-old living in Station Street, Longport (Arnold Bennett's 'Shawport') less than 200 yards away from the main-line station. Our house was a double-fronted shop near the corner of The Square. The Square was triangular, rising literally to the canal bridge at its apex where on one side was a small pottery, shops on three sides of the lower half made it a convenient local shopping centre and there, a single-track tram-line became a loop allowing trams to pass. A tall decorative Victorian gas-lamp stood alongside, on a small circular pavement.

Living near a railway station in those war years had the advantage of providing an early warning of impending air raids. At night after dark, it was reassuring to hear the noise of shunting wagons and crashing metal buffers, or the occasional whistle of an engine. Mother would say, "We are safe to go to bed; there will be no raid tonight. Men are working at the station goods-yard." It was when everything was still and hushed, when there were no sounds of shunting wagons or whistling trains, that people were afraid. Afraid that news of an impending air raid had been telegraphed to the station where work had stopped and lights extinguished. One day Mother took me to neighbouring Tunstall where we saw on a spare piece of land, a crater caused by a stray bomb from a Zeppelin. Our backyard separated us from a row of well-built Victorian terraced houses stretching down the street to the station. I used to sit on the backyard doorstep; a very good vantage point to see the strong, sturdy railway horses pulling cartloads of shells from the munitions factories, down to the station goods-yard.

I wondered if all those shells were bombs like the one dropped at Tunstall.

I was sitting there one day when the station bell rang. Hung outside the signal box at the level-crossing, the bell warned of an approaching train.

I jumped up and ran! The white wooden gates were beginning to close, but as usual I knew I would be there before the train drew into the station. My favourite place was to stand at the gate in the corner close to the platform entrance; from there, both platforms were open to view. I had been there when trains full of soldiers had passed through. Some people said they had seen snow on the coaches bringing soldiers from Russia, but I had never seen that. It was a myth. I had often seen people on the platform hugging and saying goodbye to soldiers going back from leave and as the train left the station I saw soldiers leaning out of windows looking back and waving.

Sad was the day when a soldier crossing the railway line from one platform to the other was hit by a train and instantly killed.

In the distance, the train was approaching and the ticket collector was walking toward this nearside entrance to take up his position. Now, with the fearsome noise of hissing steam, the smell of smoke and hot oil, a giant locomotive slowly came to a stop at the end of the platform, just on the level crossing where I was clinging to the railings within an arm's length, it seemed, from the locomotive's massive driving wheel. High above me, the driver was leaning out from his cab waiting for the guard's signal. With a deafening burst of steam, the monster stirred and throbbed into thunderous life. The driver smiled and waved to me.

The gates began to swing back into place with me still hanging on for the ride; my feet on the bottom stave. Before the signalman in his box on the opposite side of the crossing could see me, I jumped off and ran away.

A newsboy with papers under his arm had come into the street yelling "Speshulextraspeshul!" Folk were coming out to buy the 'Sentinel' newspaper's special edition of November 11, 1918.

The Armistice had been signed at 11 o'clock.

The war was over! The news spread rapidly and by teatime Station Street was alive, noisy and colourful. Men and women were dancing, hugging and singing! Children were prancing around waving miniature flags! An empty horse-drawn railway cart that not long before had been carrying shells, turned into Station Street from the goods-yard. The uniformed driver brought the horse to a standstill and began to lift children onto the cart. Someone grabbed me and hauled me up with the others. I found myself dumped against a little girl who seeing I had no flag to wave, offered me hers.

Then the driver, walking alongside the horse's head, paraded the cart loaded with flag-waving children back and forth along Station Street and around The Square to the cheers of the crowd.

The war was over! We were unaware on that day that when those children came of age some would be drastically involved in another world war, myself included. However, for now:

It was Armistice Day November 11, 1918.

The First World War was over!

** ** ** **

I was born on 28 July 1913, the year before the outbreak of World War I. We were then living in Brook Street, Longport, near to the canal, the gasworks, and within 70 yards of the railway goods-yard and stables; a not very salubrious area.

My earliest memory is of sitting outside the front-door on the pavement edge, eating a sandwich of bread and Condensed Milk, listening to the whistle of trains and the clash of shunting wagons.

Almost opposite was a very short street, virtually a cul-de-sac, leading into Clarence Street and the busy Station Street. Wesley Chapel was the only building along one side, with three terraced cottages on the opposite side; the chapel entrance was just around the corner in Clarence Street.

I was the youngest of five children born to William and Esther Ball - Thomas; Esther May; William Enoch (Bill); Alice Mary (five years my senior); then Albert.

I was baptised and christened in that Wesley Chapel. My parents intended having me called 'Albert,' obviously not after the famous war pilot Albert Ball VC as some folk later thought, nor after Prince Consort Albert. Nothing so pretentious!

They simply named me after my Uncle Albert.

The minister holding me in his arms ready to baptise said: "Name this child!" At that moment, my godmother whispered to mother "Call him James!"

James was the name of her baby son who had recently died.

Mother whispered to father and I became 'Albert James.' Through the years, Mrs Poole was truly a godmother and I am proud of my name.

** ** ** **

The story of 'The Runaway Horse' was family saga.

Around the corner from Brook Street was a cobbled street. Running its whole length on one side were the railway stables, a windowless building with one large double-door at the far end. On the opposite side was a boundary fence, solidly built of old wooden railway-sleepers standing upright, closely together; beyond which was the main Manchester/London railway line and the station goods-yard. The fence was thoroughly creosoted and on a hot day you could smell the creosote from our front door.

At the same time every day, old Mr Turner the stableman passed our house. He had retired from more active railway service years ago, yet still wore his old uniform peaked-hat and still held shares in the Railway Company. Ten-year-old brother Bill once asked him, "May I come with you?" At the end of the visit, when he had actually swept the wet cobbled-stoned floor with a heavy stable-broom, he asked if he could bring his younger brother to see the horses, promising not to take him too near.

Bill took me in my pushchair.

We were half way along the street when he heard the clanging sound of heavy hooves inside, a different sound from the friendly one he knew so well. He had always regarded the pawing of a restless horse in its stall as a friendly greeting to a human passing in the street; but this was different. It was a wild, clattering sound that travelled the length of the stables. Bill was afraid.

At the far end of the building a runaway horse charged out of the open door and turned down the street which was deserted except for us.

The huge snorting animal galloped along the pavement towards us, massive head high in the air with ears flattened back. Bill let go the chair to run away but immediately grabbed it again, determined that he would fling us both out of the way as best he could. Sparks fired from the broad iron shoes as the horse flashed over the stones.

Suddenly, the charging animal swerved from the pavement towards the centre of the road and passed by as though we had no existence. A stable-boy came chasing down the street followed by old Mr Turner, hatless with sleeves rolled up to the elbows, his speed hindered by a rough apron of sacking tied around his thighs. The old man shouted to Bill, "Take your brother home!" Bill turned the chair around and pushed me home.

Mother explained the danger of a runaway horse and how we might have been killed.

When asked, why did the horse run away she spoke earnestly: "Perhaps something frightened it, or it just broke loose to run wild. Sometimes the powerful things man has tamed get out of control. Then there is great danger. You were brave. Always be brave."

For some reason he could never find words to explain and for which no explanation was needed, Bill cried.

* * * * * *

Chapter 2
Board School

When father became the Warehouse Manager at the Malkin Tile Company, we moved from 28 Brook Street to 19 Station Street, a double-fronted shop near the corner of The Square. Two steps at the front door led straight into the shop where a long counter formed a passageway to the door of the living-room on the left. It was a large room and had a large front window matching the shop-window in size. Entering, you faced a Yorkshire-grate fireplace with a sizeable mirror above the mantelshelf. Whenever the insurance-collector called, he always stood on the hearth facing the mirror admiring himself as he wrote up his book. He intrigued me! He had a sharp waxed-moustache and a brown trilby hat, still on his head.

On the right of the fireplace, were cupboards and drawers in rich dark pine. Pride of place on the opposite wall, was a two-manual harmonium with pipes, pedals, and stops, to which my sister Alice, would sometimes on the spur of the moment leave whatever she was doing, to play a ballad or the latest popular song before going back to finish whatever she had left. She could not read a single note of music but played everything by ear.

The kitchen was almost as large as the living-room. A window overlooked a backyard which separated the shop from a row of Victorian terraced-houses stretching down to the railway station and in the yard was a back-door entrance with a step down to the pavement.

From thereon until I was nine years old, I attended Longport Board School, just around the corner from the Square, on the main road to Burslem and Newcastle-under-Lyme. At morning assembly, Mr J F Bond the headmaster, read passages of scripture, some of which we had to learn by heart; for example Psalms 1, 8, 23; 1 Corinthians 13; and Isaiah 55 from verse 6, 'Seek ye the Lord while he may be found.'

The school had separate playgrounds for boys and girls and separate entrances; but classes were mixed. One day, a young attractive supply-teacher was in charge of our class. In the geography lesson she put a large coloured map of Norway and Sweden on the blackboard.

Turning to us, she asked brightly: "What does that remind you of?" No answer! "Come on, tell me!" she said. Still no answer! "Well," she said with a smile, "If you don't know, I'm not going to tell you." I felt funny inside because I thought I knew what she wanted someone to say.

As the school was on the main road it was an adventure to run out from the playground to place a halfpenny or penny coin on the tramline, wait in the playground for a tram to run over it, then dash out to collect the enlarged and flattened-thin coin. However it often disappeared, stuck on the tram wheel.

Miss Veneables, a teacher in our day school was also our Sunday School Primary superintendent, an excellent teacher and an admirable person but, stubbornly, I refused to attend Sunday Primary School because I felt that we had enough of her at day-school. My parents never compelled me to attend, yet one Sunday afternoon waiting at the school entrance was a long-bearded old Wesley Chapel saint, in black frock coat. He picked me up, carried me into the Primary room, dumped me down on a chair, bent over me and loudly commanded, "Stay there!" He left without a word of apology to Miss Veneables for the intrusion.

That was the only occasion I attended Primary Sunday School.

There were more than 100 scholars in the whole school and the tradition was that new clothes should be worn on the School Anniversary Sunday. That presented quite a problem for some parents who could not easily afford to buy new clothes at any time. About 60 children were trained for singing on the Stage, (a stepped wooden platform) built each year around the pulpit for the occasion. It was a satisfying sight for parents to see the Stage full of their shining-bright and well-dressed children. The church was crowded to capacity for each of the three services. Being one of the youngest, I was seated on the front row and by the time of the evening service I was so tired that during the sermon I went to sleep, with my head resting on the knees of the boy behind me.

Sermon finished, the collection taken, time now for the final item with choir and children - the mighty choral-march!

The organ began the introduction.

Harry Hassall, the well-liked choirmaster and conductor, gave the signal for the choir and children to stand, but he pointed to the boy behind me to remain seated so as not to disturb me; to the delight of the congregation. The full force of the choral march awakened me and struggling to my feet I was embarrassed to find that folk in the front pews of the gallery were looking at me and smiling.

At the end of the day Mr Hassall always gave a sixpenny-piece to every child on leaving the stage. I received mine, but they could never persuade me to go on the Stage again!

Our recognised family-pew was in the gallery just left at the top of the stairs. Through the Georgian windows of the west wall one could see the green hillside of Chatterley Wood, with Longbridge Hayes hamlet in the valley. On a summer evening with the sunshine flooding through the windows, the smell of polished-wood and warm pitch-pine, the soft sound of the hamlet church bell, the occasional silence, the music, the lulling droning sound of the preacher's voice, as from afar, the comfort of the close physical presence of mother and the family, all gave me a sense of what I, at that tender age, thought heaven might be like.

As I grew older I occupied the end seat at the pew door.

Doorkeeper!

Sometimes there was a special service with guest artists and on one occasion, there was a visit of a child elocutionist. I was about eight years old at the time. The girl was about the same age. Three rows of pews circled the gallery to where the organ was central to the choir-pews and there she stood; reciting so confidently in the crowded church. Her voice was wonderful.

To me, it was miraculous - what she could do with words, in beautiful melodious tones. She was lovely! I could not take my eyes off her! Once or twice, I thought she looked at me.

It was very strange that as soon as she finished her final performance she immediately left the place next to the organ, climbed the steps between the choir-pews, walked along the topmost aisle of the crowded gallery and came straight to our pew. I opened the door. She came in and sat beside me until the end of the service when, with a smile but without a word, she went back to her parent. Unbelievable! Amazing! What a girl! Yet it all seemed so natural! For quite a while afterwards I suffered some chivvying from the family about attracting the girls.

I never saw her again.

A year or two after moving into Station Street my parents allowed me to walk alone up the hill to Burslem for a Saturday afternoon cinema matinee.

I liked the comfortable 'Coliseum' an old variety theatre. Sometimes I went to the nearby Palace where I saw Charlie Chaplin with Jackie Coogan in 'The Kid.'

One day, mother took me to Trentham Gardens, the home of the Duke and Duchess of Sutherland. They had recently and hurriedly left, reputedly because of the stench of the river Trent. In one section of the Hall we saw the servants' iron-bedsteads, but memory may be playing me false when I say the beds were half-made-up as though really left in a hurry.

** ** ** **

Eldest brother Thomas was a soldier in Germany. He came home on leave, so father arranged for a family photograph to be taken at a professional photographer's studio in Burslem. Tom, in uniform, was seated between mother and father, Esther and Bill stood at their rear, Alice sat at mother's knee and I stood in front of father with my hand resting on his knee. I couldn't understand the feeling of solemnity; even Esther who was always so happy, had no smile; and I did not like being dressed-up in my dark velvety-like jacket with trousers ending below the knee; I preferred my red jersey and short black trousers.

Brother Bill seemed always to be the lucky one of the family. For example, on a family holiday in Rhyl he won a free ticket for an airplane flight over the town and hinterland before finishing with a circular out at sea. "Have you said a final goodbye to your parents?" the pilot asked jokingly. That day, Bill was lucky in two ways because the next flight crashed into the sea. Pilot and passengers had to be rescued.

Esther was a good, lovely girl always bright and happy. I liked her! She looked after me and taught me to knit – *in, over, through, off*. However, for some time she had not been at all well and was in such bad pain they called in the doctor, a tall bald-headed man who glared at me through thick spectacles and with a crisp, loud voice said: "You should wash your dirty hands." My hands were not dirty!

To Esther he said: "What is the pain like?" She pointed to where she felt the pain. "It's hurting so badly," "What's the pain like?" he asked. "Is it like that teapot there?"

What a question! 'Is it like that teapot?' Teapot indeed!

Incompetence! All he could do was to tell mother that Esther was anaemic and should be taken out of the valley to live up on the hill at Wolstanton. "The purer air would help," he said.

My parents took his advice. They found a house in Wolstanton and put the shop for sale. A farmer's son from Market Drayton signed the agreement to buy. After he took possession he brazenly told father that he had no money and could not pay. It became a matter for the Courts. For a long time afterwards, father was recovering items of cash at irregular intervals. He said the young man's wife was a decent girl who appeared not to have known.

The removal day was fascinating for a nine-year-old boy. A horse-drawn van came to the door. Two massive brown horses stood passively between the shafts with their noses in a sack hung over their heads; a removal man had given them their dinner! Three men packed the furniture and belongings into the van and then the horses' food-bags were taken off and stacked away.

The puzzling thing to me was that before the van set off, a man climbed inside with the furniture and then the doors were fastened!

"Why have you locked him in?" I asked.

"To give the alarm if anything moves or goes wrong!" was the answer.

The van set off to climb the hill to Wolstanton.

I was sorry to be leaving Longport.

* * * * * *

CHAPTER 3

The Ambulance

I was a sturdy nine-year-old when we went to live in Wolstanton. At Ellison Street School, they put me in a higher class than the one I had left in Longport and on my first day I was in a fight. I don't know how, but in the playground I became involved with a bullyboy and his three cronies; perhaps they wanted to give the new boy a 'going over.' He challenged me to a fight after school in the farmer's turnip-field at the back of the building. I accepted. That day I was wearing black short trousers and my red jersey. That red jersey always gave me confidence. At the end of afternoon school, the four boys led me into the turnip-field together with others who had heard of the fight. They stood around the contestants. The lad was serious. His blows were hard. I was blessed (according to how you look at things) with a short temper, usually under control, but when he landed a shocking blow on my nose, I lost it. I didn't hear the noise of the watching crowd but just went at it, exchanging blow for blow. Suddenly we stopped! Stood facing each other; and shook hands! The others crowded around patting our backs and we became friends, or at least not enemies. It was on a Wednesday. I know, because the boys invited me to go with them to the Wednesday afternoon matinee at the Marshlands Cinema. We were in the best two-penny seats at the back. They treated me!

At the age of three, or at the time when I could hold a pencil or crayon, I was colouring black-and-white pictures in books. I still have one book! In Wolstanton, a teacher disciplined me by providing plaster-casts for me to copy and shade in pencil. At school, for the art lesson the teacher always sent me out to the cupboard in the hall to collect the 'apparatus' as he called it; lovely brushes and splendidly smooth, black-japanned paint boxes. I liked the feel of them; and they contained proper watercolours. Up to now as I write, I have painted more than 700 watercolours, a score or more commissioned portraits in oil and have taught watercolour painting for twelve years. Although I have to admit that some may have natural talent, I have often said that anyone who can write their own name can draw. Sometimes I am asked did my parents paint.

Neither my parents nor my grandparents had the ability, yet both my elder brothers, Tom and Bill, were quite good with pencil and brush. Strange!

Art has been one world in my life and religion the other. As a retired Minister of Religion, I think I have had the best of both worlds.

One May morning, my sister Esther seemed in normal health and before going to work had laughed and joked with Bill. I liked Esther. She was always bright and happy. She had taught me to knit, you know - *in, over, though, off* - and promised to buy me a pair of knitting-needles and some wool for my tenth birthday in July. I was looking forward to that. At lunchtime, two of her workmates brought her home from work ill and in pain. Dr Horner, surgeon, who was now our family doctor in the best sense of the term, immediately diagnosed appendicitis and ordered an ambulance to take her to the infirmary.

When I came home after morning school, cousin Mavis and Mrs Heeks, the next-door neighbour were there. Mavis was warm and friendly, a regular visitor who sometimes made a special creamy rice pudding with currants for me. I looked on the table. No plates were laid. Nothing! I sensed something was wrong. "Where's mother?" I asked and ran across to my cousin who told me that mother was upstairs, Esther was ill. She has to go into the Infirmary. "Two of her workmates brought her home at eleven o'clock and when the doctor came he told Bill to ring for the ambulance."

"Where's Bill, now?" I asked.

"He went to fetch your father from work."

"Where's Esther, now?"

"Upstairs," said Mavis. "Your mother is with her. Do you want to go up to see her?" She knew how fond I was of Esther. "No, I don't want to," I said.

Mrs Heeks, a tall buxom woman always ready to help, was filling a hot water bottle. "Be a good boy," she said. "Bill and your father will soon be here and the ambulance won't be long." She took the bottle upstairs.

There was a loud knock at the front door. This could not be father and Bill, they would come in the back way. Cousin Mavis went to the door. It was father, Bill, and the ambulance. Mrs Heeks came hurrying downstairs. Mother followed and sat on the sofa at the bottom of the stairs. She was crying. I watched father go to her and as he sometimes did when she was crying, put his arm around her and said: "Don't worry, lass!" I heard Bill telling Mrs Heeks how they were just coming down the street when the ambulance turned the corner. They stopped it and came with it otherwise the ambulance would have been here before them.

I stood by the open kitchen-door and watched Bill go out to the men who were bringing in a stretcher. Father had gone upstairs. Cousin Mavis was sitting with mother. "Don't worry, Ma" said one of the men to mother as they brought in the stretcher. "We shall soon be bringing her home again." Mother began to sob.

At the kitchen-sink I filled a cup with cold water and drank the cupful. I did not feel hungry but had the same feeling in the stomach as when I had eaten too much chocolate; it was funny because I had eaten nothing. Out in the backyard, quietly passing the kitchen-window I saw the men going upstairs. I went through the gate without looking back. Isolating myself, I bore my grief alone, and running quickly to the bottom of the short street stopped at the corner, to hide. I was sorry. I did not know to share my sorrow or that sorrow was common to mortals.

Peeping around the wall I saw a small group of neighbours standing outside the house. The ambulance was there with the doors wide open and I watched the men carry out the stretcher covered with a red blanket.

I was sorry I had not stayed with Esther, but I did not like ambulances - or funerals. Whenever I saw a funeral approaching I would run down the nearest side-street until it had gone by.

They recalled too vividly how Vera, one of my Longport school playmates, going home from school one day caught sight of her brother and ran across The Square to him. I saw the heavy steam-lorry go over her and remembered the ashen face of the driver and his trembling hands.

I remembered her funeral.

It seemed a long time before a man, wearing a cap like a bus conductors, closed the ambulance doors, climbed into the cab and drove away. The neighbours went away from the door. I crossed over to the opposite pavement and walked, hands in pockets, slowly up the street. The kitchen door was closed. I listened to the voices in the kitchen. All women's voices! I heard the rattle of plates.

My dog Charlie had been tied to the kennel. I patted his head, opened the door and walked in. "Where've you been?" mother asked gently. There was no tone of reproof. "Come and have your dinner. You'll be late for school." Mrs Heeks gave me a favourite, a banana-sandwich and shortbread biscuits. Then off I went to school.

Esther died next morning, aged twenty-one. An abscess had burst on the appendix. Peritonitis had set in.

I suppose it is true to say that my parents never got over the shock.

My birthday came and went. I thought about Esther. I thought about the knitting-needles she had promised. Someone remembered and bought me a pair of knitting-needles and some wool and I knitted a scarf as she had taught me, *in, over, through, off*. I was very fond of Esther. She was so good, so bright and happy.

* * * * * *

Chapter 4

Stoke Wakes Week

At Wolstanton Ellison Street School just before my twelfth birthday, they coached a few of us for a scholarship examination which Mr Phillips, my teacher, expected that I should win. I prayed earnestly for success! When he announced the names of the three winners, mine was not one of them! I could not understand it. It just could not be! The surprise and disappointment was impossible to describe. I was devastated! I should now have to remain in this top class until I left school at fourteen. Miserable thought! However, one morning a week later as soon as class assembled Mr Phillips, looking at me called out my name. I stood up. "Stand up on the form," he ordered. I climbed on the bench wondering that he was about to punish me for something? He then turned to the class. "There has been a mistake in the scholarship marking," he said. "Albert Ball has won three scholarships, County Minor C, County Minor D and Wolstanton Free Place." He led the applause. I have never forgotten that incident and never shall. When I later visited the school, it was a thrill to see my name in gold letters on the Honours Board.

Stoke Wakes Week was the time in August when the Potteries-folk took their annual holiday and Station Street, Longport, became a very busy thoroughfare. The down-line platform was crowded with passengers waiting to go to the North Wales coastal resorts; my mother and I, setting off to stay with Uncle Fred and Aunt Gerty at the Lye near Stourbridge, were among the few on the up-line platform.

Over the road from the Lye Cross Memorial on the corner of Chapel Street was the Temp Cinema, originally the

Temperance Hall; next door was the police station, with its blue gas-lamp marked 'Police'; on the opposite corner was the Council Offices building, then the Congregational Chapel beyond which, on the widened pavement standing back a few feet, were a newsagent's and a hairdresser's shop. Mother turned into to a narrow tunnelled-entry between the two shops. I followed. "Where are we going?" I asked. "You'll see!" She laughed.

I did see. Sunlight and colour splashing roses and carnations, gladioli and delphiniums, marigolds and geraniums, aquilegia and moon pennies, in an old English garden and a centre path leading up to a double-fronted cottage standing proud and secluded, the Stourbridge-brick glowing a warm ochre in the afternoon sunshine. Honeysuckle and wisteria framed the door and windows. It seemed to me the oddest thing that this was the only approach to 98 Chapel Street!

A very old lady wearing a long black dress and white apron was sitting on a chair at the open door. To a boy, she looked 'the ancient of days.' A smooth-haired fox-terrier came skidding down the path followed by Uncle Fred, sleeves rolled up to the elbow and wearing an open black waistcoat over a striped-apron. He greeted us heartily and carried in the luggage. Aunt Gerty, a tall, buxom, rosy-faced person with dimpled cheeks was putting finishing touches to the tea laid out on the table under the window. The cottage had a cosy smell of newly-baked bread. She welcomed us with warm hugging embraces! After the grown-ups had finished their greetings, "Well, child," said the very old lady with the long black dress and white apron, "bain't you going to say a word to your Aunt Polly?" New to me was the South Staffordshire sing-song drawl and the pervading smell of lavender.

After tea, Uncle Fred showed us what the terrier would do at his command. He put a scrap of newspaper on the tiled hearth and set a lighted match to it. "Put it out, Floss!" The dog quickly stamped out the flame with her front paw. "Birds in the garden, Floss!" She was away in a flash, barking up-and-down the path. The best was when he told her to fetch the evening paper from Riley's newsagent shop at the bottom of the garden. She returned with it in her mouth and released it to no one but Uncle Fred. "Floss is well known in Chapel Street," said Aunt Gerty. "You should see her when she's sent to the grocer's, carrying a basket in her mouth and comes back with the bread. When the postman comes, he waits at the bottom of the garden and whistles for Floss to fetch the mail."

All this was so delightfully new! It was like being on a discovery!

Sleeping arrangements were very new! The first bedroom was an open space at the top of the stairs which Aunt Gerty and mother would share. You had to walk through to the door of the second room, Aunt Polly's bedroom. Uncle Fred and I had to share a bed put up in the front parlour.

During that first night, a bad dream caused me to rear up in panic and scream.

Dazed, I saw a face on the pillow next to me and leaning over began stabbing a pointing finger towards it, shouting "Who's this? Who's this? Who's this?" Uncle Fred awoke, raised himself and gently putting an arm around my shoulder, spoke very softly, "You're all right. You've been dreaming. Lie down. Go to sleep. You're all right." Next morning, all I remembered was seeing a face on the pillow and shouting, "Who's this?" Nothing of the dream!

The first day was for exploration. The small adjoining building with its moss-covered, slated-roof was a wash-house. Fascinating! It was cool and damp inside with a clean earthy smell. In the far corner was a round, built-in copper boiler on a small fire-grate opening, an old pump did not work but an iron mangle with a large, splendidly decorated handle did.

The rear base of the cottage was a few feet below ground so there was no back-door. Instead, in the wash-house there was a small opening in the wall with fastened boarded-shutters. I had to climb on a chair to open them and was then eye-level with a field. I managed to get through and was in a little paddock, where a friendly brown pony came trotting towards me. During the holiday, that paddock became a playground and the pony soon knew me.

The grown-ups set limits to free exploration. They permitted Albert Street and Union Street but High Street and the vicinity of the Lye Cross were out of bounds.

Explorations with Uncle Fred were adventures.

There were lovely long journeys on those wonderful Midland Red buses. I had never seen such splendid buses, the length of them, the lovely red colour of them, my favourite colour! There was a seven-mile journey on an electric-tram to Kidderminster through the lovely countryside. I could not remember what was to be seen at Kidderminster other than Uncle Fred's shoe-shop, because the tram-ride interested me most. Then there were the rock-dwellings at Kinver, and the amazing crooked house at Himley where you put a bottle at the bottom of a sloping table and watch it roll up to the top. All very odd!

The sights and sounds of Chapel Street were satisfying too. I liked to sit on the pavement at the bottom of the entry, watching and listening. Men came into Cockrayne's for a haircut or a shave and there was the occasional glimpse of Mr Cockrayne lathering a customer's face. Sometimes a woman lathered. That was certainly new. I wondered at that!

There was jolly laughter and shrieks of children playing in the road outside the Union Inn. One girl stood looking my way then left them to walk over to me. "Why don't you come to play with us?" she asked in the sing-song drawl with the tone-lift at the end. She was a bright-eyed girl. "I don't know anybody. I don't live here," I said shyly. "Doesn't matter where you live! Come on!" She grabbed my arm and pulled me to my feet. "No, I don't want to." "Oh, all right then." She let go and ran to join the others. Why did I refuse? It is too late now but if she came again I would go. She was lovely!

Uncle Fred was proud of his garden, now so rich in colour. He taught me how to layer carnations with a penknife and wheat seeds. I was always tempted to touch things, to feel their texture and shape and where possible to hold an article in my hands. "Don't touch! Keep your hands away," said mother. "He baint a'doing harm Esther," wheezed Uncle Fred. "Leave him be. He may be doing something wonderful one day with his hands, a surgeon or the like."

The Sunday evening was a quiet, peaceful evening. I was in the garden. With the Chapel wall on one side and a high dividing wall on the other it was quite secluded. I listened to the muted sound of organ music and singing from the chapel and recognised the hymn tune. Father was a Wesleyan lay preacher and I was accustomed to attending church. Now, I had a very strange feeling that I could not understand. The organ music and singing came to me somehow in vivid colour, the garden colours were all intensified and for some inexplicable reason, standing there in mystic solitude, I had the feeling that I too would become one of Wesley's preachers.

Across the street there was a cottage, converted to a shop with the small window full of things for sale. The shop was special! I liked the large coloured metal sheet advertisements, like 'Cadbury's Chocolate' and 'Coleman's Mustard' crowding the wall.

On Monday afternoon there was a matinee at the Temp and I was tempted to smoke a cigarette in the cinema where I wouldn't be known.

I walked up-and-down past that shop-window hesitating to go in for a packet of Woodbines.

I nervously plucked up the courage. The doorbell tinkled as I entered and I could smell paraffin-oil. The shop was empty. I stood waiting at the counter so long that I turned around intending to escape just as a tall man came in from the kitchen-door. Leaning down over the counter he stared at me, wide-open eyes magnified behind the spectacles with thick lenses. I put two pennies on the counter and asked for a packet of five Woodbines. "How old are you?" Overpowered I could not answer. "Little boys shouldn't smoke!" He continued to stare.

My legs began to tremble and I wished I had never gone in. Then he turned away as though to go back into the house. From a corner-cupboard he took the cigarettes, brought them to the counter, gave them to me, picked up the two pennies and growled: "Tell them not to send you for them in future." In a hurry, I almost fell outside, but in my pocket was a box of matches and five precious Woodbine cigarettes in their thin green-paper-packet with the open top. I was confident now to smoke a cigarette in the Cinema.

Inside, there was the warm smell of plush seats, old carpet and stale tobacco smoke. With a struggle, I managed to light and smoke a cigarette. I smoked the remaining four, one a day, in the washhouse making sure the boarded-shutter was wide open. There in the Lye, I smoked my first cigarette. There in the Lye, I had a premonition of what I was going to be, a Methodist minister.

* * * * * *

2

INDUSTRY

Chapter 5

Anthony Connelly

September 1925 was the year I won the scholarship which gave me a start at the 'Orme Boys School' Newcastle-under-Lyme where all was so different, with chairs and separate lidded-desks instead of forms and benches. Most of the Masters wore gowns in class and the school had a motto, '*Medio Tutitimus Ibis*' - The Middle Way is Best. The simple uniform was a black cap with a pearl button on the top and a silver rampant-lion badge attached on the front. Weather permitting, the whole school walked three or four abreast to St. George's Church for morning assembly where the headmaster, Dr Rutter, conducted the short service and our music teacher, Spencer-Jones, played the organ. He was a rotund, jovial man wearing the lapel-badge of the 'Froth-blowers Association' a brilliant organist who often improvised during his voluntaries, sometimes to our delight including occasional snatches of popular songs.

My first Art master, elderly Mr Jordan, was a favourite. Others were Mr W Bullough my form master, his subject German. H G Lane, witty and sarcastic, taught History. He once told me I had 'brains like a piece of old shoe leather' about which incident I reminded him years later at a Rotary Club dinner. He was a pipe smoker with a second pipe always ready charged. Others I could name - Mr Crinson, a young Geography teacher; B K Davies, Maths and English. One master I won't name, was generally disliked in our form. He often came in normally, but at other times in a fearsome rage; at those times we needed to be careful. He was a giant of a man and would often pick up a piece of chalk and throw it hard across the room at an offending boy. It was said he had suffered from shell-shock!

Arnold Bennett attended the school when it was 'The Middle School.' I am a member of the 'Arnold Bennett Society' and recently sold 47 of his works from my library, including a number of first editions. In 1913, the year of my birth, he had three plays running concurrently in the West End. My wife, Dorothy, told me I was a fan only because I lived in the Potteries and he had attended my school. Partly True!

My first form 2A was held in a Methodist Church schoolroom across the road from the School building which was not large enough to accommodate all the pupils, so a new school was built in Milehouse Lane, Wolstanton and in 1929 the Orme Boys School became the 'Wolstanton County Grammar School.'

It was officially opened on October 4th by Sir Oliver Lodge, DSc FRS. My parents were invited and I still have the invitation card.

My reports from both schools showed that throughout the whole time, in every term except two, I had been top of the form in Art; so it seemed right and appropriate that here in the Potteries I should follow my natural bent. On leaving school I started to work at 'E Roddy & Son, Fall Birch Tile Company, Hanley' as a Tile and Fireplace Draughtsman and studied at the 'Burslem School of Art' under Gordon Forsyth.

One September Thursday afternoon I followed Ernest Roddy upstairs to the first-floor Drawing Office, which was just above his ground-floor office at the front of the building. Anthony Connelly was standing at a large drawing-board painting a landscape on a 12" x 36" panel of 6" x 6" white tiles. "Good afternoon, Connelly," said Mr Roddy, holding a lighted cigarette. "This is Albert. He's going to do some drawings for me. Look after him and help him get set-up." He rested the cigarette between his lips and wrinkled his eyes against the rising smoke. A chain-smoker!

Anthony Connelly was a stout man of medium height, his slight grey hair parted down the middle gave a benign look to his generous features and a charming smile dimpled his florid cheeks; a heavy watch-chain spread in two loops across his fancy grey waistcoat. He peered over the top of gold-rimmed spectacles and fixing his brush between his lips shook my hand, murmuring something inaudibly.

"I'll bring Tom Mason up shortly to show you what to do. Let me know if there's anything you want. My office is just below," said Mr Roddy as he walked out.

I went over to the old artist. "That's good," I said, watching the effective brush-strokes on the almost-completed painting of Lake Killarney. "You want to know why I'm doing this trivial stuff. I'll tell you why lad! Food, bed and shelter, nothing more and lucky to get that."

With a slender palette-knife and a rapid circular movement of the fleshy wrist he mixed up more pigments and flicked each blade of colour on to his palette. "Lord, how good youth is," he said aloud. He used the last drop of turpentine from a sticky green bottle and was handing the bottle to me when suddenly, flaying his arms and mahl-stick in the air, he pushed me aside roughly and stamped madly to-and-fro cursing furiously. I stepped back quickly towards the door in amazement and waited.

The outburst ended abruptly as it began. "What is it?" I asked. "What's the matter?"

"It's Thursday afternoon, lad! The shops are closed and I've no turps."

He set down his tools, drew his stool to the fire, lit his pipe, took up his newspaper and started to fill in his weekly competition. "Ever won anything?" I asked. "Heaven knows I've no wish to win a fortune but if I could only get enough money to live on, I'd paint what I like; not that trivial stuff." He looked at me and began openly to soliloquise about his early days. Anthony the boy, running out very early on a summer morning to do his pencilled studies of tree- trunks and roots before doing his house-chores that freed him for school.

Things were not easy in his apprentice days.

There were long hours in a pottery artists' shop, drenched with the smell of fat oils, turpentine and of aniseed oil.

Apprentices who weren't immediately at their master's beck-and-call were belaboured.

How eagerly he assimilated all they could teach him. How quickly he became conscious of his own mastery of the medium. How irresistibly he turned to painting chrysanthemums and roses, paintings that had life embryo in them, petals that developed a living texture; a dewdrop was given so much life that the undiscerning admirer would try to wipe it off the picture. Then the day came when he sold a lovely little study of chrysanthemums to a Duke and the day came when he could boast himself a gold-medallist rose-painter on Minton Ware. Adulation smothered him at the nightly assembly of his artist friends in the Angel Hotel, splashing his money about as though painting on a 'ten-leagued canvas!' Back at home, by the light of a gas flare in the attic-studio, doing another study to be sold the next day; again in the Angel at night with his friends, always spending and giving his money away.

More work, more painting, getting and spending; God, how long that went on! But the painting, what glory that was! Fusing the inanimate substance of the earth into a very similitude of life and without any right to the power that was his. His genius didn't belong to him, he said. It belonged to his friends at the Angel. It belonged to those who could pay for it, like the Duke; it belongs to the rest of men! He must give it away. He had no more right to his powers than men had the right to live. If he had, why was he now painting trivial landscapes for fish-and-chip-shop panels at eight-pence a tile? If his brother had the right to live, why was he killed as a youth when thrown by a horse?

He'd to give all he'd got, his art, his money, his knowledge, himself. "But it makes the Devil laugh, because it was a case of the poor giving to the rich," he said. "I'm painting now to keep body and soul together, and lucky to do that. But who cares for Anthony Connelly now?"

"You've been a fool, Connelly," said elderly Tom Mason who had crept stealthily into the studio as he always did and heard part of the artist's soliloquy. He was the previous owner of the Fall Birch Tile Co and to keep a position in the firm he was now the Works Manager, using the Drawing Office as his base. "You've been a fool to yourself! You could easily have been a wealthy man and you know it," he said.

"Well, you're in a good position to talk, you rich old miser. You wouldn't give a filthy pipe away." Connelly re-lighted his pipe and held out his pouch: "Here, have some tobacco." Mason refused, and returned the offer from a flick-open tin. Connelly's cheek dimpled with the smile, a gentle whimsical smile.

While Mason was advising me about drawing records, about books of quantities, about the type of drawings and paintings required, Connelly folded his paper and began really to study the competition. Half-an-hour later he put on his jacket, picked up the empty turps bottle and told us he was going across to a friend on the New China Pottery to beg a drop of turpentine.

For six years he had been filling in the News of the World competition every week. Then one day he won a cash prize and he didn't come near the studio for a month.

It was eleven o'clock one Tuesday morning; Tom Mason and I were drinking tea when we heard Connelly's heavy footsteps on the stairs. He came in smoking his pipe and hung his dirty mackintosh, cloth-cap and jacket, behind the door.

Walking over to his drawing-board, which was just as he had left it, he stripped up his sleeves haphazardly to the elbow, stood for a few moments, then turned to us and said: "Throw that stuff out of the pot and make me a nice fresh cup of tea." He sat on his stool by the fire.

"Tom Mason here, the old swine of a miser, knows I won a little fortune," he said. "And I reckon I hadn't any bloomin' right to it." His smile brought the dimple dancing in his cheek. He re-lit his pipe, took a few puffs before saying: "Now, I'm back where I was."

That was in September.

In November I was taken ill. I lost the use of my legs. Couldn't walk! I was in bed for sixteen weeks and at one point was said to be critically ill. Mr Roddy sent his son with my wages on Friday evenings. Doctor Horner said it was "a nervous breakdown affecting the heart." He regularly visited me. He also regularly admired an upright tile panel I had painted, a winter landscape on three 6" x 6" tiles, so much so that when mother offered it to him he readily and happily accepted. Subsequently when I was up and about, he invited me to his home to see the framed-panel on his sitting-room wall. He had already promised my parents that he would sponsor me through Kensington College of Art, all expenses paid.

I did not accept the remarkably generous offer because when I was twelve, I had made a covenant.

Years later, a clever Tideswell doctor, Dr Brookes, thought the symptoms of that illness as I described them to him, indicated a polio attack.

When I returned to work I had the Drawing Office to myself as Anthony Connelly now rarely came in. Ernest Roddy was a bulldog breeder with kennels at Basford. Not wishing to leave her with his kennel-man he regularly brought a Crufts champion with him to the office and because my office was upstairs and quieter, he brought her up and asked me to keep an eye on her. She was aptly named *Basford Cinders* - she would lie close up to the fire-grate with her nose almost in the ash-pan.

He frequently came up to sit talking with me while 'handling' his dog. A good rapport developed with my boss. Fortunately also with his dog! One day, instead of *Basford Cinders,* he brought another much younger dog, also a champion soon to be shipped to America. A day or two later I had an intercom call to go to the factory slabbing-shop about an intricate fireplace design. When I returned I found the Drawing Office door open and no dog! Immediately I rushed down to Mr Roddy thinking he had fetched her.

He hadn't! The dog was missing! We searched the factory to no avail.

He went in his car searching in one direction. I walked the other way into Hanley, my heart beating wildly. In the town centre I spotted her. In the grassy centre of a busy traffic island she was standing motionless, frothing at the mouth. Risking life and limb I dashed across through the traffic, picked her up and carried her all the way back. She was very heavy! My jacket was covered with froth!

We discovered that one of the warehouse girls had come up to the Drawing Office for a 'quantity list'. Opening the door she saw the bulldog coming towards her, turned and fled leaving the door open. The dog followed, walked downstairs and out at the open front door into the road, unseen.

Ernest Roddy was very understanding about it all, but as far as I remember he didn't bring another bulldog to work.

Throughout my married life we always had one or two dogs. We started with Jane, a wire-haired terrier. One Tuesday she was due to have puppies; but because it hadn't happened before bedtime we prepared her basket in the attic and went to bed.

In the night she came downstairs and jumped on the bed with a cleaned-up puppy in her mouth to show us. Clever girl! I took her back upstairs and Dorothy was midwife to four more puppies.

Through the years we had terriers, a corgi, a poodle and finally bulldogs. Dorothy bred from the terriers and the bulldogs. Our experience is that when you've had a bulldog, you won't wish for any other breed. One could write a chapter about their nature, their lovely-ugliness, their idiosyncrasies and above all their loyalty. The breed has a sorry history. I feel it is trying to eradicate itself because they are rare; difficult to breed.

However, talking about dogs has taken my story many years ahead of itself.

* * * * * *

3

COLLEGE

Chapter 6

Brothers

In 1933 I became a Methodist Local Preacher in the Burslem Swan Bank Circuit. (The Superintendent Minister's Manse was 295 Waterloo Road, once the home of Arnold Bennett.) In 1938, after eight years experience in industry, I entered Hartley Victoria Theological College, Alexandra Road Manchester, an accepted candidate for the Methodist Ministry. In my first year the Principal, Dr W L Wardle, a notable Hebraist was President of the Methodist Conference and was often away from college. In my second year I was one of five students he selected to do Hebrew with him.

I spent the1939 summer vacation as an excursion-leader at the Brockley Hall holiday-home Saltburn-by-the-Sea. When it became clear that World War II was about to start, guests departed and for me it was back to college with all the wartime restrictions! The St John's Ambulance Brigade trained students in First Aid to certificate standard and we were all registered Air Raid Wardens. The college cellars became air-raid shelters for the use also of nearby neighbours.

During the 1940 summer vacation I worked on the local Assistance Board, Newcastle-under-Lyme, investigating Old Age Pensioners' means-tested claims for Supplementary Pension.

Early one morning I called at the home of brothers Fred and Joe Soames; an interesting visit which I wrote up in my journal as 'Brothers'. It seemed that I had disturbed them, as they said, from "settling down after breakfast for half-an-hour before starting morning chores." Fred answered my knock on the door. Joe was sitting in his rocking-chair by the fire lighting his pipe, but turned in surprise as Fred brought me into the small living-kitchen. "The investigator from the Assistance Board," he told his brother. "From wheer?" asked Joe.

"He's come about thi pension," replied Fred.

Joe brightened. "Sit tha down, lad," he said. I pulled a chair up to the table, drew some documents from my briefcase, took a fountain pen from my pocket and turning to Joe I asked: "Are you Mr Fred Soames?"

"No, theer's Fred." Joe nodded towards the window where Fred had re-settled on the sofa. "Then you are Mr Joe Soames! I've come to see you both about your claims for supplementary pension and have brought some forms for you to sign. First, I must ask you a few questions and I shall want to see your pension books."

"Fred, get th' pension books," said Joe. Fred went across to a chest of drawers that occupied most of the wall opposite the fireplace, rummaged in the top drawer among Co-op divi-checks and old gas-bills until he found a book. He put on his spectacles and examined it intently. "That's mine," he remarked, placing it smartly on the table. "Wheer's yours?"

"Tha stupid," growled Joe. "Keep thi specs on and have another look. It's allus kept in th' top drawer." Fred raised his spectacles above his eyebrows and further scooped through the divi-checks, some fluttering to the floor; "Ah tell thee it isn't here," he said. "Well, look in th' middle drawer," was the reply. Fred looked in the middle drawer. He searched diligently with no result and turned a questioning eye on Joe.

"Look in th' bottom drawer, tha fool," said Joe, but before Fred opened the bottom drawer he said, "I know wheer it is! I left it on th' window-bottom after I drew th' pension. Tha should 'ave seen it, sitting theer on th' sofa. A lot of good thi specs are." Fred quietly handed me both books.

I continued the investigation with a number of questions and was satisfied with the answers. Then came this one: "Are you married Mr Soames?"

"Who, me?" asked Joe. "Yes."

"No. Ah'm a bachelor."

"And you?" I said, turning to Fred. "He's a bachelor," snapped Joe.

"Single. Both 'n us," laughed Fred sheepishly. Joe glared at him.

"How much rent do you pay?" was the next question.

"Thi questions are getting a bit personal, aren't they, lad?" said Joe. I explained that before an application could be considered it was necessary to know the circumstances of the applicant, to know if there was real need.

"Well, Ah think it's a cryin' shame. All this fuss about an extra bob or two." Joe tugged at his moustache.

Fred answered the rent question.

"How much money have you in the bank?" was the next question.

Joe threw down his newspaper, knocked his pipe on the hob, rose from the rocking-chair and stamped around the kitchen. He poured out a furious tirade. He was very abusive. "Impertinence! That's what it is. Impertinence! What right have you, nobbut a youngster, to come here asking me questions like that?"

He expressed many opinions about the government, the Assistance Board, and quite a few newly-formed ones about the investigator. I patiently reminded him that he was the applicant for the extra pension and that as investigator I was only doing my job of work when I asked such questions. In any case, every applicant could have a certain amount of savings before it made any difference to the case. "If it is less than a hundred pounds you need have no fear in declaring it," I told him. "Ah'll never tell how much Ah've got," declared Joe.

"All right. But if you are not going to tell me, it means that the Board will not be able to consider your application. It is left entirely with you but as I say, if you haven't a lot of money in the bank..." "Joe, tell him how much tha's gotten," Fred burst in, evidently discomforted. He stirred himself up and down on the sofa, 'like a cat on hot bricks.'

Joe stared at his brother. He brushed a forefinger quickly back- and-forth along his upper lip to straighten his moustache, took a deep breath and puffed it out expressively. What he intended to say in a following outburst is not known.

He restrained himself and walking back to the rocking-chair picked up the newspaper, lit his pipe and said no further word. Fred willingly gave information concerning his own savings. "Ah've nowt," he said. "Not a penny."

Joe disdained any further question, so I asked Fred to sign his own application. He pulled down his spectacles and signed, testifying that the information given was true to the best of his knowledge and that he was aware of the penalty of making a false declaration.

"Mr Soames," I said, turning to Joe, "I shall be in the district again tomorrow and will call to see if you have changed your mind. I hope I shall be able to complete the form." "He's doing his best for you," endorsed Fred.

He ignored both remarks.

On the following day, I tried to persuade the resolute Joe. "My own feeling is that you will be grudging yourself if you don't give the information about your savings. You've applied for extra pension and I expect you need it. I am only trying to help."

Joe grunted.

"If you don't wish me to know the exact amount and if it is less than one hundred pounds, say so and I will put down that statement as an answer to the question." He was even more abusive. Convinced that I could make no progress I said I would see him again in three or four week's time and took my leave.

Fred closed the middle door behind him with a sign that he did not want Joe to hear what he was about to say and followed me to the front door where he whispered: "Tak' no notice of th' owd fool. He's nobbut twenty-three p'uns in an owd tin box upstairs under his bed. Ah know, because Ah've counted it."

I smiled and wondered at the humour, the bathos and the stubbornness of some men.

** ** ** **

Manchester suffered the Blitz of 1940. We found ourselves in the thick of it when we were putting out fires from incendiary-bombs dropped on the college grounds. A landmine in a neighbouring street blew out the college chapel-window. I was then the College Secretary and spent part of my Christmas vacation helping to clear up the debris.

I understood that Hartley Victoria Theological College was unique among the Methodist colleges in having a 'Philosophy and Logic Chair'; Professor Atkinson Lee, of Manchester University. We were proud to be his students. In addition, we had a renowned tutor for Elocution - Professor Bernard, who taught the actor Robert Donat.

We left college full of hope!

******

Chapter 7

"Wrong Way Round"

My appointment on leaving Hartley Victoria College, Manchester, in September 1941, was to the North Derbyshire Circuit; to Tideswell where I had pastoral charge of the Tideswell church and six others - Bradwell, Hucklow, Litton, Eyam, Peak Forest and Sparrowpit. The author and playwright, Dr L dü Garde Peach, who lived near Hucklow said: "You don't see the glory of North Derbyshire until you've seen it in the depth of winter." My Circuit Steward told me that if I could stand the Tideswell winter I could stand any Circuit anywhere.

I cycled in the deep snows until I could get a car, which happened like this. Tideswell has a small Roman Catholic Church and the priest lived in a small bungalow in the church grounds. Father Cafferky was a friend. Petrol in wartime was rationed and restricted, so having only the one church he was unable to get a licence. He sold his car to me - a red Mini, for £30.

Maggie, a well-known character in the village, was his housekeeper.

One day he invited me for supper. I walked through the church-gates up to his presbytery and knocked on the door. Maggie opened it and I expected to be invited in. "Well?" she queried, keeping me standing at the door. "Father Cafferky has invited me for supper," I said. "The bloody 'ell he has!" A Pause and then: "You'd better come in!" That was Maggie! The cottage in the village where she once lived is now clearly named '*Maggie's cottage.*'

I conducted my first wedding in this my first appointment, at the end of my first week. Everything was arranged before my arrival so all I had to do was to conduct the service.

My only experience of a wedding had been in my very early teens when I was best-man for my sister, Alice. I was then too nervously occupied feeling in my waistcoat-pocket making sure the ring was still there to take much notice of what was going on. In theological college, there was obviously much theology-subjects such as Christology, Soteriology, Ecclesiology, Biblical Exegesis, Logic, Psychology, Greek, and Hebrew, but as far as I remember nothing on how to conduct a marriage service.

In the Book of Offices there are rubrics, general instructions printed in red. In that early Methodist Service Book it read: '*On the day and time appointed the minister shall stand, the man on his right and the woman on his left.*'

On the day and time appointed I stood there, Book of Offices open in my hand, the young couple in front of me. During the singing of the first hymn I glanced at the book, at the rubric, at the couple and again at the rubric, '*The minister shall stand, the man on his right and the woman on his left.*' The man was on my left. The woman was on my right.

Oh dear! What to do? What I did was to lean over and tell them to change places, which they did without a murmur. I now had the man on my right and the woman on my left, which seemed to me what the rubric said. Better? Worse! The church had a centre-aisle and under the window at the far end stood the caretaker. They called him 'Thrafty' because he was always complaining about the church being draughty. He was purple in the face, grimacing at me. However, all went well until the putting-on of the ring when it appeared to me the couple was all at sixes-and-sevens.

At the end of the service, I led the bridal party to the vestry for the signing of the registers. Standing at the vestry door, his face now a reddish purple, was 'Thrafty.' He stormed at me, shouting: "You've wed t'em t'wrong way round." I said: "I know." The reproof was merited. So, my first wedding; and I had married them 't'wrong way round.' I thought afterwards that if the marriage should go wrong they would blame me.

Many years later in 1975, a new Methodist Service Book was published. The ambiguity of that troublesome rubric had been removed and now read: '*The persons to be married stand together the woman on the left hand of the man in the presence of two witnesses.*' That was clear, but I do not think for a minute that the revision was solely due to my wedding experience all those years before.

However, I noticed that they had left out any mention of the minister.

Many years later, published in 1999, the Methodist Worship Book tells the couple not only how to stand but where to stand. '*The persons to be married stand together before the minister, the woman on the left of the man.*'Another improvement, but I am not sure that is unambiguous! '*Before*' may be spatial or temporal. It is not unknown for a minister to be late for a wedding.

In the 20th year of my retirement, I conducted my last wedding. Those involved wished it to be an informal one and I gave an informal address.

I recounted the experience of my first wedding and followed with: "I think in some way I am reminded of the text in chapter eight of Paul's great letter to the Romans – 'All things work together for good to those who love God' (Romans 8:28). The Greek word for 'work together' (sunergei) can bear the meaning, intermingle, 'All things intermingle for good to those who love God.' Worse things remain the worse. The best remain the best. Nothing changes. They don't fuse together like the ingredients of a cake, they remain the same.

Past mistakes, sorrows, failures, regrets, the painful events all remain; they have happened, they don't change. They are not obliterated but by God's grace they intermingle with the better things, the achievements, the joys and successes of life and make something which is altogether good. 'All things intermingle for good to those who love God' is a message of Hope.

The themes of the marriage service are love, hope, faithfulness, sacrifice and trust, all values at the heart of the Christian Gospel. In the service, the two are each asked the question; "Will you love, comfort, honour, be a companion through all the joys and sorrows of life?" The answer is, "With God's help I will."

There are and will be joys of life, of real heart-warming splendour. Baron Von Hugel, a great theologian, spoke of seven truths of the soul (or psyche if you prefer the word) the seventh was JOY, the ultimate, the chief end in life.

That is the ideal but being human, most of us meet up with the sorrows and the troubles, yet by the grace of God joys and sorrows intermingle to produce a synthesis - a life of rich experience which is altogether splendidly good, full of the high values Beauty, Truth, and Love. I believe and have believed for a long time, that all things work together for good.

If I needed any consolation for the botch I made of that first wedding it would be in the form of a letter I received from the bride and bridegroom of a wedding I conducted soon after my retirement. I have it before me now, written on wedding notepaper. May I quote?

Dear Albert,

Thank you very much for the excellent service you conducted for us. We received many presents, but yours was the most precious, and one that we shall never forget. You used beautiful words, and put us both at ease; I think every one enjoyed it.

Thanks again.

As I have said, I believe and have believed for a long time that *All things work together for good to those who love God"*

** ** ** **

Again, this has taken me many years ahead of myself.

Back to that first week in Tideswell!

The villagers were telling me so often what I ought to do that my hair bristled at the back of my neck. It seemed the one thing

I ought to do was to go to see the Play at The Hucklow Village Theatre. Dr L du Garde Peach had converted an old barn, or as he called it 'an 18th century lead-mining cupola' into a theatre with 265 seats, a stage thirty-feet deep and a sixty-feet auditorium. He put the Plays on at the time of a full moon to make it easier for patrons travelling along dark country lanes.

I did not go to see the Play at the Hucklow Village Theatre.

Thereby, I missed a wonderful opportunity of sitting in the crowded Hucklow Village Theatre and of seeing the Tideswell girl-star.

Dorothy Hall, in '*Fantasticks*', by Rostand.

CHAPTER 8
Dorothy Hall

In his book *Twenty-five years of Play Producing 1927-1952,* Dr L du Garde Peach wrote about Dorothy Hall: - 'Our next performance was in June, 1940, a month which few people in this country are likely to forget. The Play was Shaw's *Caesar and Cleopatra,* which for ten years I had been wanting to put on the stage at Great Hucklow. The only thing that prevented me from doing so, was the lack of a satisfactory Cleopatra. Now at last I had found her.

'I had gone to a local production of some play, I forget what, but it was a miserable affair, in which unsuitable players seemed to have been thrown together by chance and produced by nobody. It was all pretty grim, until suddenly a girl came on to the stage whose performance stood out like a flame. At once I forgot the shoddy production and saw only her. Marianne's reaction was the same. She turned to me and said, 'There's your Cleopatra!' After the performance had come to a merciful conclusion, I got hold of her and asked if she would like to play at Great Hucklow.

'She was moderately interested, but the more I looked at her, the more I was determined to have her at least for one production. She *looked* just right for Cleopatra and I was already convinced that, given the proper production, she would be able to play the part. She agreed to come and read it at an audition.

'If ever there was a natural little actress, it was Dorothy Hall. She didn't have to be *told* what to do; in fact, if you told her, she got it wrong. Instinctively, most of the time, she got it right, whether she understood it or not. Quite often she didn't.

But it made no difference to her performance. She had all of that something which it takes: She made the audience listen to her.... I shall never forget her first appearance as an actress with the Village Players. When the curtains opened on the scene with Cleopatra nestling between the paws of the sphinx in the desert no Caesar ever found a more attractive little minx of a Cleopatra waiting for him. Dorothy played the scene perfectly."

He wrote later, 'Dorothy has star quality.'

On his 80th birthday, L du Garde Peach was interviewed on TV about his theatre. The only picture he put on the screen was the black-and-white photograph of Dorothy Hall as Cleopatra 'nestling between the paws of the Sphinx.'

I have that picture, framed, in the entrance-hall of my flat.

Dorothy Hall's grandmother (Granny) was a member of my Tideswell Fountain Square Church, where during the war years the ex-Primitive Methodist church in High Street, united for Sunday Evening Service. One evening in the crowded church I saw Granny Green in her usual pew, but sitting next to her was a wondrously attractive girl whose presence stood out, as Laurie Peach had said, 'like a flame.' It was her granddaughter, Dorothy Hall.

I was fortunate to have lodgings in Bank Terrace with an ideal landlady, Mrs Norman Hill, a widow with three sons; two married, one in Liverpool and the other in Darley Dale. The youngest son, Stafford, was in the Eighth Army in Africa: She treated me as a mother towards a son. She lived to the age of 104 years, having survived a cancer operation when she was eighty. The two married sons told me an amusing story. They took her to Blackpool Illuminations for an exciting, enjoyable day's outing. They said they gave her a 'real treat.' Back home, they asked her how she had enjoyed it. "Oh well" she said. "It's passed the day on!"

The back-gate of her Bank Terrace house was in Alma Road, which climbed steeply towards the moor. On the right, about fifty yards higher up was 'Ivy Cottage' where Granny Green and family lived. Not many days after that Sunday evening service, I was surprised to receive a note from Dorothy Hall inviting me to a musical evening in 'Ivy Cottage' where she would have friends; Mr Armstrong, the headmaster and his wife and Alex Wilson, the village chemist, a member of the Hucklow Village Players (about whom the Manchester Guardian theatre-critic had said that Alex was the best amateur actor he had known.) Dorothy was at the piano. She was a good, expressive pianist and had a most sensitive touch.

At that time, she was a student at the Royal Academy of Dramatic Art having won, at Dr Peach's instigation, the Leverhulme scholarship. Her granny told me she was having difficulty in finding suitable lodgings in London. The Academy had warned her and one or two other students to move away from where they were staying, as a girl had been murdered nearby.

I wrote to Dr Donald Soper at the Kingsway Hall seeking his help. He kindly let me have some addresses; but meanwhile Dorothy's uncle from Worthing had a situation in London and she was able to stay at his place.

* * * *

When my College Principal, Dr Wardle, suggested the Tideswell appointment for me, he said that a country appointment has its advantages, "You won't have so many women's meetings to attend and you'll have time for your probationary studies." Coming from a city like Manchester, after three years in college with about 80 men, to a quiet village like Tideswell, brought a touch of melancholia. The appointment was for four years.

Theological Students were exempt from conscription to War-service but I had offered for a Chaplaincy and was awaiting a call to a selection committee.

In Tideswell, I was the Billeting Officer to oversee the placement of evacuated children and I also received official denominational notifications. One such was to inform someone of the death of a sailor-son who had been killed.

I discovered that his parents attended the Anglican Church, so I went to the Vicarage with the letter. It was a matter for the old Vicar who had the reputation of sometimes coming to take his church services in a half-drunken stupor. Be that as it may, he was very well-loved in the parish.

That day I learned an important lesson in pastoral psychology.

The parents lived in the adjoining 'Vicarage Cottage' and the vicar sent for the father to come round. A slender grey-haired elderly man walked in, erect and dignified. The old priest, after greeting him, walked towards him, handed him the letter and said: "Your son has been killed."

Just like that!

The old priest told him to sit down. The father read the letter: then stood up quietly and facing his vicar, said no other words than "I must go and tell his mother." They shook hands, firmly gripped and then he left.

The vicar ordered coffee for us and explained his method of breaking sad news. "It's no good trying to soften the blow by saying something like: Sit down now, don't get alarmed. I've some sad news for you. Don't get upset! Keep calm!" That sort of thing only makes matters worse. In normal circumstances it's better to tell the news outright, straightway; they are not worked up and are better able to stand the shock."

Next to the Vicarage gates in the Market Square was a large house standing back with a straight drive between well-kept lawns up to the front door. It had the appearance of a country hall. I called it, 'Hatter's Castle.'

It was the home of Dr Brookes, the village doctor, who was renowned and trusted as a clever doctor. (He previously had a practice in a mining area and he told me some harrowing experiences of mining accidents he had attended). He was also somewhat eccentric. It had been known for patients to be sitting in his waiting-room a considerable time, while through the window he could be seen leisurely feeding hens in the garden. He was known to make home-visits at very late hours, sometimes around midnight. Very interested in Art, a collector of Peter Scott's bird-pictures, he regularly kept his eyes open in patients' homes for any picture that appealed to him. He was also interested in my Youth-club work and came to its productions.

I had attended a Youth Club Leaders Residential Course at Repton School, and started clubs at Tideswell and Bradwell churches. I suggested to Alex Wilson, the village chemist and active member of the Hucklow Village Players that he should produce a pantomime at Tideswell, to which suggestion he readily agreed and produced 'ALLADIN' a successful week's performance, in which I played the Emperor. I received professional make-up from Dorothy Hall. Fifty years later, I met a man who told me he had remembered something I said all those years ago.

I had the hope it would be some 'pearl of wisdom' I had quoted from a sermon or other. He laughed! "As the emperor in the Aladdin pantomime, you said to your servant Mustapha – Mustapha, I mustapha drink."

Oh well!

The next Tideswell Youth Club production was '*SEASONS FAIR,* a Pageant of Song, Music and Eloquence, naturally in four Acts: Spring, Summer, Autumn, Winter.' Dorothy Hall made an appearance! We had a smart, capable boy as Stage Manager and very efficient he was. He became a professional actor; later a BBC Producer - Bill Sellars. He invited Dorothy and me to see him at the BBC where he took us on the 'Dr Who' set. I like to think it was my asking him to stage-manage 'Seasons Fair' that set him off on his career.

In December1940, Sheffield was blitzed on three nights, 12th, 13th and 15th.

For a brief respite Rev William Wallace, superintendent of the Sheffield Methodist Mission, came to the North Derbyshire village Eyam, to the home of Jabez Ollerenshaw, a stalwart of the local church and Circuit.

It was perhaps because of Jabez Ollerenshaw that after having done only two years of my appointment at Tideswell, William Wallace seconded me to work with him at the Victoria Hall Methodist Mission in Norfolk Street, Sheffield.

However, the Victoria Hall had a congregation of 2,500 every Sunday evening.

So there was work to be done!

Up to now, I have not said anything about the other North Derbyshire churches in my pastoral care. In Bradwell, I formed a Youth Club. Fifty years later, some of those young people were leaders and stalwarts in the church.

In Litton, I went with my Society Steward studying bird-nests in the valley. Great Hucklow had only about two-dozen homes but some very interesting, and friendly people.

In Eyam, one young church member became a Deaconess.

In Peak Forest, I named a newborn calf.

In Sparrowpit, under a harvest moon, I helped a farmer get in his hay.

All this, in addition to taking planned preaching-services and official meetings in all the villages and making many friends; as well as braving the snows.

And before I left Tideswell, I was 'walking out' with Dr Peach's 'little flame'

Dorothy Hall, his star actress!

* * * * * *

Chapter 9

"Dreams Come True"

Commandos invaded Sheffield! Parsons attacked the Steel industry! Individual Works Management and Unions agreed to have chaplains and some specially requested them. We were unpaid, part-time Industrial Chaplains in the Methodist Church before the time of the Sector Ministry when Ministers could become full-time Industrial Chaplains. Rev Bill Gowland, who later formed the Luton Industrial College, was one of the Campaign leaders. (In 1959, I drew a caricature of him which was published in the Methodist Recorder when I was the Recorder's first cartoonist. R G Burnett was the editor.) What the Commando Campaign meant for me was a weekly visit to a crowded Works-canteen to give lunch-time talks to men at their meal and I felt sure that not all of them appreciated having a parson interrupt their meal.

Rev William Wallace (Bill) campaigned in the pubs and there were some remarkable results. The Salvation Army had been visiting pubs for many years with their 'War Cry' newspaper.

I learned much from William Wallace! He was the superintendent of the Sheffield Victoria Hall Mission, a powerful and persuasive preacher with charisma. He surely had something special to hold a congregation of 2,500 every Sunday evening in wartime. He was able to forge good relationships with the Civic Authorities, the Chamber of Commerce and social organisations. He had a good sense of humour; "Never ask a woman's age directly," he once advised me. "Always say, how old are you because you don't look it."

The Victoria Hall, on the corner of Norfolk Street and Chapel Walk, is a red-brick and stone building with an imposing tower. The main entrance is in Norfolk Street but its normal weekday entrance is in Chapel Walk, a narrow pedestrian shopping-passage from Fargate to Norfolk Street. It was built on the site of the Norfolk Street Wesleyan chapel of 1786, demolished in 1906.

My room was at the far end of the gallery on the Chapel Walk corner of the building. One could hear the constant clip-clop sound of women's high-heels below on Chapel Walk and the traffic noises of Norfolk Street. I can still recall that clip-clop sound.

In addition to the day-to-day practical church work during our four-year probationary period, tutors assigned essays for us to write on given books and I found time to do these essays more easily in quiet Tideswell. However, essays had to be done but there was always the temptation to take a break, to go downstairs for a chat with the office staff, or to go across to Davy's restaurant in Fargate for a coffee; or for a stroll around the city. Stephenson Square was interesting. There was a row of ten tall, red telephone-boxes lined up outside the General post Office and the King Edward statue, which was unveiled in 1913 the year I was born, stood boldly in the Square, A News Cinema was also another temptation.

Victoria Hall had an excellent Youth Club. One large first-floor Lecture Room had been equipped with beds as a hostel. For a charge of one shilling, servicemen travelling through Sheffield could have supper, bed and breakfast with a wake-up call at any time in the night if they needed to catch a train. Girls from the Youth Club did the catering voluntarily and the staff took it in turns to be on duty. It was exhausting to work through day, night, and day without much respite. Normally there was no trouble, but I was on duty one night when after all had quietened, a soldier came into the office and told me that there was a coloured America GI sitting up in bed holding a knife, threatening to murder someone, "He's keeping us all awake." In the hostel I found most of the men awake and in the far corner-bed, the coloured American soldier was still holding a large knife, still muttering. I went to phone the American Military Police. Back again in the hostel I judged it best not to approach the disturbed, threatening soldier but sat on a bed talking with two or three of the men until the American Military Police arrived. They took the lad calmly and gently away, without any restraint upon him or any resistance from him.

That was a scary episode! It was the only time in my hostel experience that anything untoward had happened. Some splendid and courageous men passed through that hostel. I remember talking with a happy dark-skinned American GI who said his principal was that wherever he went, especially in someone else's country, so to conduct himself that he could return with a clear conscience.

When I came to Sheffield I stayed first at the home of Mr and Mrs Watson, active members at the Victoria Hall. Mr Watson was the Boy's Brigade captain. I was grateful to Mrs Watson for her care when I had an attack of flu, which kept me in bed for some days. She was good! Dorothy Hall visited me there, as she did when to be nearer the Hall I changed lodgings to Abbeyfield Road, a nearby residential area, where Mrs Reilly, a returned missionary, a refined, dignified lady lived. Her husband had been an Army Chaplain and from their rich experience she gave me some helpful information. And his army Sam-Browne belt which I wore when I became an Army Chaplain.

I was involved with the Wybourne church. It was built at the time when Rev Benson Perkins was the Mission superintendent and it was built in the wrong place! This small all-purpose building was in the isolated lower-end of the estate nearer the city, instead of higher up in its heart. Yet it had a small congregation of kindly, saintly Wybourne people. The young folk perhaps, had their problems but two or three capable young people from the Hall came along to help.

The estate was the result of the Pond Street slums-clearance, when families from the crowded back-to-back, closely-packed houses with outdoor-toilets were given newly-built houses with bathrooms, in a garden-estate. Good as it was to have the chance of better surroundings; one important quality of life was taken from them and sadly missed - neighbourliness.

Previously, they could stand in their backyard and talk to a neighbour over the wall, or call in a close next-door neighbour if help was needed.

The two Deaconesses at the Hall, Alice and Phyllis, did most of the pastoral visitation in addition to their work in the ladies' meetings and other groups. In addition to making tea for the V I P s.

I found time to write up in my journal one pastoral visit I made and it was later published in the magazine 'Prediction'. Having had the Editor's written permission, I will include it here. 'I met Mrs Gill when she was boarding-in university students. She had as many as four students lodging with her at a time and sometimes gave them hospitality without taking a penny from them.

"Folks think I'm crazy," she said. "But I can afford it and it gives me pleasure. This is a large house and if I lived alone I should have to shut off some of the rooms. I may as well make use of the place." Although her husband had died some years ago, Mrs Gill is not a *poor lonely widow.* She is wealthy and generous, making the best of her loneliness.

She and her husband were very much alike, knowing instinctively what each would think and say in many given circumstances. They even had the same dreams at the same time. When she told me this, I thought immediately of Freud and Dunne, of wishes and sex, of broken time-sequences and symphonies.

"When the same dream comes to two people who are very much alike it is sure to come true." After a number of such experiences Mrs Gill maintained the conviction.

Telepathy in wakeful consciousness, I thought, so why not telepathy in sleep, as well as foreseeing the future? Prof Dunne wrote - 'In sleep the strong chain of the consecutive moment-by-moment of our wakefulness is broken and in this relaxed consciousness there is freedom to find the unified reality of past, present and future, to find a universal oneness.'

Mrs Gill's harmony with her husband, her 'old Dave' was a small part of her harmony with the whole universe, linked by a universal relation to all the cities and continents of the world, linked to all who are now writing or talking, listening, or sleeping, playing or dreaming, linked to all past generations and all future generations. One's self, extended into one whole Present which is Unity.

She missed her 'old Dave'. They had lived so much in harmony that she expected him to come back to her. He has not done so yet, unless one comes back in dreams.

Before her husband died, they made plans to buy a lovely little bungalow at Cliff End, where they spent most of their holidays camping. Dave loved the place. He always said he would like to settle down at Cliff End, so they found a bungalow for sale and had everything arranged to buy. They even had the date fixed with the solicitor to make the final transaction and saw it all beforehand in one of their dreams. What amused them afterwards when they described it was the owner of the bungalow. He was funny, with his fiery red beard and blue eyes; a tall man dressed in a rough tweed suit and a Sherlock Holmes cap. Dave called it a 'poacher's cap.' And he carried a briefcase under his arm. They dreamed they bought the bungalow from him and settled in. Dave had built a workshop, which he said would do for a garage.

That was what they dreamed.

However, about a week later, they actually saw that 'old red-beard' when they were shopping in the town. He was standing at Cole's corner, as though to cross the road. "Look, Lil," Dave said. "Look who's there!"

He had the same red beard, blue eyes, tweed suit and briefcase. He gave Mrs Gill a hard stare as they passed, as though wondering whether to speak. She regretted not asking if he had seen her somewhere before, perhaps in a dream.

Everything was arranged for a final settlement and the date fixed for a meeting with the solicitor when her husband died. A fortnight before the date!

"That was trouble, if you like. I didn't know what to do. I wondered whether to go ahead and buy the bungalow or not. I wondered what Dave would wish me to do. Sometimes I stand quiet and still and say, Come on Dave. Tell me, what shall I do?" She thought he would have liked her to buy; so she decided to go on with it. It was at this point in Mrs Gill's story that I pointed out to her that the dream did not come true. "But you *did not* buy the bungalow," I said.

"I laugh many a time when I think about it," she replied. "The day before the appointment, I dreamed I was in the solicitor's office and there, sitting at the desk was our blue-eyed red-beard. The same eyes, beard, suit and the briefcase! But he wore no cap. He had thick hair brushed well back. I remember laughing at him in my dream. He put the papers before me on the desk and handed me his pen. I remember taking it and was about to sign when I looked up to ask whether to put my full name or my usual signature and there, standing behind him, stood Dave.

He was waving his hand sideways, to and fro, telling me not to sign. "Dave" I said, "You here! What do you want?" I remember mouthing the words and making no sound. I laugh many a time at the blank amazement on red beard's face, as he turned round to see who was there. Of course he saw no one."

"So you *did not* buy it," I said.

"No. I believe Dave came back to advise me. I believe in dreams," said Mrs Gill. "When two people have the same dream it is certain to come true."

"But you both dreamed you had bought the bungalow and went to live in it. *That did not come true*," I declared. "Of course not, lad," she said. "That was because my old Dave died and it couldn't. It would have come true had he lived."

** ** ** **

Soon after that visit, I received a letter requesting me to attend the next Selection Committee of the Royal Navy, Army and Royal Air Force Board of the Methodist Church, to be held at the Central Buildings, Westminster, London.

Obviously, they interviewed the candidates singly and from what one of them said afterwards, as well as the more serious questions there had been lighter ones. "Are you engaged?" asked one committee member. "No sir!"

"Oh well," was the reply. "We'll soon find you a nice little WAAF."

The Committee consisted of uniformed officers from each of the three Services. After a few questions, they asked which Service I wished to join.

"The R A F" I said without hesitation. "Why R A F?" asked one.

"I prefer the uniform."

That started a lively debate among them, each arguing for his uniform as being the smartest and best. I escaped with no further questioning!

I received a letter telling me they were delighted to inform me that the Committee had decided to offer me a Chaplaincy when I could be released from my Circuit. That I was to be heartily congratulated on my selection and that I would still be under the discipline of the Methodist Church and will have to pay the normal Connexional Assessments.

They assigned me to the Army! I was now an Army Chaplain!

My medical examination took place in the pavilion of the Sheffield Bramhall Lane cricket and football ground. Eyes were tested by a kindly man who for a moment was suspicious that I had a squint. When I came to the psychiatrist, he plied the usual questions about my medical history, hobbies, until he learned I was a Methodist Minister and closed the questionings with a smile, "You should be inquiring into the state of my mind not me enquiring into yours."

A considerate clerk took me to the recruiting officer to have my application-form completed with my medical grading, A 1 (One). They gave me a railway travel-warrant for an interview with the Assistant Chaplain General (ACG) at Military Headquarters, York.

After a delightful interview in the York Cavalry Barracks with an officer who had been dealing with men in the Army for over a decade, I felt reassured. The barracks was a training-depot for recruits. A band of the regular Army had 'played in' a column of soldiers returning from ten-mile route-march. As we watched from the office-window the Staff Chaplain said, "You wouldn't think, to look at them, that they were raw recruits only five weeks ago. Civilians, who came here all shapes and sizes with their long hair and slouching carriage, now are soldiers!" And they were! All very smart! With a healthy outdoor-tan on their faces. Such was the result of training and discipline!

I would get my next instructions from the War Office and the probable date for calling-up would be September 16. Because I was now an Army Chaplain my Ordination was brought forward to that year's Methodist Conference. It should have been held in London but by reason of Hitler's doodlebugs, it was transferred to Leeds. My parents came to the Ordination. Dorothy Hall was now in the Army: conscripted from RADA into the ATS. She had a compassionate posting to a Holding Company in Matlock, N.Derbys. Her mother had been a WAAF in France during the First World War and her uncle, George Green DSM, was killed in 1918, a commander of a battery of six guns.

At the end of July I said goodbye to the Sheffield Victoria Hall and to civilian life. I bought my officers' uniform and cassock at Henry White's of Newcastle-under-Lyme and spent August between my home in Wolstanton and 'Ivy Cottage' Dorothy's home in Tideswell, before going to an Army School in Tidworth; to train for my job as Chaplain to His Majesty's Forces.

There would be a fortnight's training.

A mere fortnight!

* * * * * *

4

ARMY CHAPLAINCY

CHAPTER 10

Army Training

I set out from home at 7.00 a.m. on a Saturday morning for Tidworth, bordering the Salisbury Plain, a place which seemed easy to reach but which presented a difficult and tedious war-time journey. The first part was from Stoke to Derby where with five minutes to spare I caught the St. Pancras train, already overcrowded and supplemented with four extra coaches. Four hours later, it arrived at St. Pancras, which left me ten minutes to catch the 12.50 to Tidworth from Waterloo. I gave up the idea but did take a taxi to Waterloo where, at the refreshment stall I met Griffiths who had travelled from Northern Ireland and had been on his way since four o'clock Friday afternoon. Our instructions were to catch the 12.50 to Tidworth and report before 5.30 p.m. We caught the 2.50 and reported at 7.10, twelve hours after I had set off from home.

At Waterloo, we were two late ones. At Andover Junction, we were three, Tom Job having joined us. Tom was from St Giles, Newcastle-under-Lyme. By the time we reached Tidworth our number was five.

A sergeant took our luggage and after a few minutes walk, we reached the Royal Army Chaplains Department (RAChD) Reporting Centre and Depot where we had interviews with the Commandant, Colonel Woods (Bishop of Lichfield's son) and his assistant Rev John Arthur; afterwards, another interview with the Assistant Chaplain General (ACG).

Our sleeping quarters were huts just opposite the Rectory. There were six beds. We each had the use of half a wardrobe and a chest of drawers. Dinner was at 8.00 pm! Quite good! After which, there was an introductory talk by the Commandant and then to bed.

Next morning was 'Documentation' - two hours of filling forms, cards, documents etc. some for permanent custody at the War Office. It was Sunday, the afternoon was free and as we were the only ones in for tea, Tom Job and I had a tray in the Ante Room. We looked through the Group Photographs of previous Schools and I was happy to see in different groups, some of my college pals, Clifford Sutton, my clansman, looking as bright as ever, Clifford Chesworth, another clansman, Ernest Verrill, Ronald Jobling, and Fred Harland, my predecessor at the Victoria Hall.

After a stroll over the hills to see the glorious expanse of the Downs, we had supper and so to bed, the end of our first active day in the Army.

Next day, after various lectures, at 1400 hrs. (Continental clock now) they issued us with equipment. Gas-cape, respirator, eye-shield, anti-gas ointment (two tins), battle-dress, towels, socks, plate and mug (tin), knife, fork and spoon, jack-knife, kit-bag and steel-helmet. That occupied most of the afternoon. After tea there was an interesting hour's lecture on Army Organisation, which left us dizzy and reeling.

The Physical Training exercises on the lawn after breakfast every morning were not very arduous, but made me aware of muscles I never knew existed. Throughout the fortnight, Physical training was an important feature with regular cross-country runs; we were now doing exercises which in the first week would have been beyond me. More and longer cross-country runs! On a beautiful September afternoon I enjoyed a run that was tough; up Windmill hill, down by the Fir Copse, across the road by the cemetery and over the hill to the Depot. The remarkable thing was that three weeks ago it would have been impossible for me to do it. Now there was no consequent muscle stiffness.

After supper on Wednesday, Tom and I went to the RTO (Railway Travel Office) to enquire times of trains, as his wife was hoping to come at the weekend. On our way back, we passed various large barracks occupied by Americans who seemed to disregard blackout regulations. There was a show in progress at the Garrison Theatre but the doors were locked. We went into the Hippodrome cinema and although it was 2130 hrs. we were shown two seats. The house was crowded with American soldiers and I saw only one woman in the audience. The film was 'The Woman of the Town!'

On Friday, the Order for the Saturday afternoon exercise was put on the notice-board. Tom now knew his wife was definitely coming from London to stay a few days in Tidworth. Dorothy Hall would also be here for the weekend.

Saturday reveille was at 0630 hrs. After breakfast, they issued us with web-equipment and rations - four sandwiches and a piece of cake, wrapped up in newspaper. The second rendezvous was fixed for Sally Lunn's Cottage where we would get pots of tea and cake 'on the Mess'. The 'grandfathers' set off at H hours. The next pair was at H + 8 and the others at eight-minute intervals. We were the third pair and set out with an improvised map-case in hand and our steel-helmets.

The first rendezvous was at Windmill Hill ridge, where John Arthur was waiting for us and where, supposing we were lost, we had to make plottings and compass-readings to find our position on the map. We set off again and came to Cleburne Wood where we tracked through on a course of 15° E of due N.

Eventually, we reached the clearing where we were to leave the wood. Then on for the last part of the route to Sally Lunn's thatched cottage, a delightfully-arranged eating-house in the quaint old English village with groups of thatched cottages and wells in front gardens. From Sally Lunn's, I hitch-hiked to Andover Junction to meet Dorothy on the 2.20 from Waterloo. She arrived at 4.20. At Sally Lunn's we had omelette, toast and cakes with tea.

On a walk over the Downs Jock joined us. Jock was a stray camp-dog full of fleas, a black cairn terrier that persisted in coming with us and spent the evening with us. Dorothy was a dog lover! We left him at the Police Station overnight.

Dorothy stayed overnight at the home of Mr and Mrs Rumbles. After dinner, we collected the dog and set off to Andover Junction. On the 2.19 train, packed to the doors, we had to stand all the way to Waterloo, a matter of two-and-a-half hours. At 5.00 p.m. we were dashing down to the Tube, Dorothy carrying her case and I carrying the dog. We were at St. Pancras with five minutes to spare. I bought a dog-ticket and a few sandwiches for Dorothy, who would have no opportunity for a meal until 10.30 pm. I dashed back to Waterloo and rang the George Hotel, Tideswell, for a taxi to meet her at Millers Dale Station. I arrived back at Tidworth at 1020 hrs. having had to stand during the whole train journey.

On the second Wednesday, we were given instructions about reporting at our appointed Command. The ACG (Assistant Chaplain General) of my Western Command was a Methodist, Rev H J Basham and the address was The Old Rectory, St. Mary's Hill, Chester. At the foot of the instruction paper 'on reporting to a Unit' were words of advice in parenthesis: *(Don't let your transport go till you know where you are to sleep)*. I liked that!

On the last Friday, a lot of 'spit-and-polish' was used in preparation for the visit of the General Officer Commanding (GOC) Southern Command, a Lieutenant General. Criticisms of his dress, made later by the men, showed that we had learned something during the Course:

(a) His Sam-Browne belt was over his shoulder-strap. It should be under.

(b) He wore it in the Officers' Mess. The belt should not be worn in the Mess but left in the Ante-room. However, he was GOC and probably above such rules.

At 1630 hrs. we reported for a briefing for the day-and-night exercise. The intention was; more physical exercise and practice in map-reading by day or night.

We were given seven map-readings. At three of the places we would find a tin box containing a paper to be signed with names and times of arrival. The first pair set off by bus to Bulford Post Office at 1725 hrs. The next two pairs at 1740 hrs. Tom and I were the third pair. Seven minutes after the second pair had gone we started on a 14 miles course across field and meadow, cultivated land, roads, fences, through ditches and woods, trusting to our ability to read compass and map. We reached the first objective at a cross-track and signed our names on the paper, which had these injunctions: 'Sleep on now and take thy rest' and 'Arise, let us go hence!' It was dark before we reached the Quarley Hill wood where the tin box was at the Bench (an obelisk for purposes of surveying). One danger point we crossed was an electrified-wire surrounding a field of cattle. "Nothing to worry about gentlemen - you just step over it." In the wood, we were lost for fifteen minutes. Consulting the map by the light of a torch we tried to estimate direction and bearing, but there was neither moon nor stars, only a 'blinkin drizzle of rain! Uncomfortable, to say the least.

The walk up to now had some compensation. We passed through a delightful old English village before coming to Three Corner Hat, a triangular road-island surrounded by trees.

However, our difficulties had only just started. Tom walked 50 or 60 yards one way, while I went the same distance the other way but we could not find a Bench, in fact nothing more than a telegraph pole. Our intention then was to cut through the wood to the North East, which is what we did. However, when we did come into a clearing we were on the same side and within fifty yards of the spot where we entered it!

In a last desperate determination, we decided to circle the whole wood. Having gone about a hundred yards, we heard voices. To the right of us were the Commandant and John Arthur standing at the obelisk. John gave us each a refreshing sweet! The first pair of men, the pathfinders, should have left a tin but had apparently lost themselves.

The second pair only had reached that spot a quarter of an hour before we entered the wood. This was half the journey done, and it was turning to rain.

With the assistance of the Commandant, we got our bearings again and set off for the last seven miles. Skirting the wood over the roughest bit of country yet, we reached a place where the barbed wire fence was broken down. Tom and I were walking side-by-side and together realised too late that we had reached the wire. In one second, Tom had stumbled flat on his face and in the next second, I too was flat on the ground!

The next objective was Hill 565. We never reached it!

On a main road about a mile before reaching the hill, Tom suggested we hitch it back to Tidworth. His heel was giving him trouble. We had barely decided when a bus approached and stopped for us. About three-quarters of a mile down the road we came to cross-roads where we caught a bus for Tidworth, arriving at the Depot at 2215 hrs. A good shower followed by a hot supper of shepherd's pie, with peaches and rice pudding as 'afters' revived our spirits. And so to bed! I had walked a distance of ten miles over hazardous terrain. Good work pal!

So, after a fortnight of many lectures on Army Organisation, the Chaplain's Function and Duties, King's Regulations, with much emphasis on physical training, we were all physically fit and mentally conscious of being in the Army, in the Royal Army Chaplains Department.

Tom was posted to Eastern command. I was posted to Western Command.

To

19 ITC (Infantry Training Centre)

Formby, Liverpool.

* * * * * *

Chapter 11

Gold Or Platinum

Arriving at 19 ITC (Infantry Training Centre) Harrington Barracks, Formby, Liverpool, I followed the guidance given at the Chaplains Training School, Tidworth and reported, first to the Adjutant then before letting my transport go, I made sure of a place to sleep - Formby Golf Club, which the Army had requisitioned. At dinner that night in the Officers' Mess, the Adjutant introduced me and in the next few days I met Company Commanders and Staff in their various offices. Finding my way around the Barracks, I became acquainted with the men and their routine duties; I was gradually becoming used to Army life. The Regimental Sergeant Major was a formidable person. Even young Subaltern Officers could feel intimidated. You needed permission before entering the Sergeants' Mess.

When I left the Victoria Hall Sheffield there was a Sunday evening congregation of 2,500, here there was twice that number of personnel including a few girls of the ATS for whom I had no pastoral responsibility.

Thousands of soldiers must have passed through Harrington Barracks.

Padre Griffiths, the Church of England Chaplain, became a good friend. He could be courageously outspoken at times and I remember sitting next to him at Dinner one night opposite Major R... For some reason an altercation was going on between them. I must admit the Major was not very popular. For example, he had a punctuality obsession. If he booked a driver for 1800 hrs. and the driver had arrived a few minutes early, he would send him away and order him to report promptly at 1800 hrs. Each night in the Golf Club he would demand his bath at precisely the same moment, regardless of others.

A chaplain, on first joining the Army, has the equivalent rank of Captain with three 'pips' on his shoulder-epaulette; a Major (next rank up) has a 'crown'.

The altercation ended abruptly by Padre Griffiths saying, "Report to me in my office at 0900 hrs. in the morning." It amused me! What a hope! As if the Major would!

My office was equipped with the basic Army furniture and a telephone. A round, coal-burning iron stove about three feet high, provided the heating, its metal flue rising through the ceiling. It was not very elegant, but efficient in cold weather and sometimes too efficient.

"I'm going to be married," said Pte Heywood when he came to my office one morning.

"Well, that's not a bad idea," I said. "Congratulations! What's the girl like?"

"She's rather lovely sir. Here's her photograph."

From the inside battledress-pocket he took the wallet. His bright blue eyes lighted joyously as he handed me the picture. I thought; *this photograph should help to keep him straight when he gets overseas*. "How old is she?"

"Twenty!"

He replaced the photograph as carefully as a child putting a coin in a purse. His soft, fair hair made him look not much more than a babe himself'. "How long have you known her?"

"About two years. I would like your help, sir." I was apprehensive, wondering if the lad was about to ask me to marry them. "What can I do?"

"It's a matter of the wedding ring. I'd like us to get married proper like, but I can't afford to buy a ring."

"That's rather important, isn't it," I volunteered.

"Yes, it wouldn't be fair not to get her one... I wondered if you, being the Padre like..." he hesitated modestly, "might have a fund I could borrow the money from."

"I'm afraid I've no fund that would serve the purpose and I don't know of one. Ask Major Hughes! There may be some Company Welfare fund..."

"But I thought you would have helped me. I promise I'd pay it back."

His problem was naïve; but he seemed genuine.

"How much do you want?" My knowledge of the current price of gold or platinum was limited; I assumed they would be soaring. "Four pounds," he said eagerly. "Is that all? Can you get a good wedding ring for that?"

"Well, sir, the one I have in mind would satisfy her."

I had already concluded the lad was honest and felt that if four pounds was all he needed to buy the ring, well that wasn't much. Although I wasn't sure that marriage at this early stage of his army career was a thing to encourage without more consideration. The lad's candour and obvious sincerity won my heart. "I'd let you have something back every week," he promised. "I should be grateful, sir."

"Very well. I've no fund at my disposal but I'll lend you the money out of my own pocket." I counted the notes. "Here you are! Is that enough?"

(I learned later that it was against 'King's Regulations' to do such a thing.)

"You get your pay on Fridays. I shall be here every Saturday morning"

"Oh, thank you very much. That's very kind."

"Remember," I said, opening a notebook and picking up a pen, "I expect you here every Saturday morning until you have paid it back. What's your number?" I wrote. "What Company? Hut?"

On the next Saturday morning I waited longer than necessary before deciding that Pte Heywood must have been on 'fatigues'.

The following Saturday I felt it would be too much of a coincidence if he were genuinely prevented from reporting. So, on the fifth Friday I went to his Company office. The Orderly Sergeant was a splendid fellow.

The crease in his sleeves and trousers was devastating. "Give my compliments to Major Hughes and tell Pte Heywood to report at my office tomorrow at 0900 hrs."

"Sorry, sir," was the reply. "Pte Heywood has a long weekend-pass. He went at 1600 hrs. today. The poor blighter's getting married tomorrow!"

"In that case, make it Tuesday morning." He came. "Well George, how was the wedding? You had perfect weather. Did you get the ring?"

"I'm dreadfully sorry sir, I didn't see you before. I just couldn't do anything out of my pay. There's been so much expense. It's a costly business getting married."

"But you did promise to pay something back each week. A small amount would have satisfied."

"I'm sorry. I'll be able to do something next Saturday."

"All right! Next Saturday and don't forget!"

Next Saturday came and no Pte Heywood. Again, on the following Friday as the sun was setting over the sand-hills, I walked over to Heywood's Company office. Sergeant Denby was late typing Company Orders that night. "Tell Private Heywood to report to me tomorrow morning." "Sorry, sir," he called out over the sheaf of papers on the table. "He was posted overseas with 'B' detachment on Wednesday."

"Oh, well! Make a note that you let me have his address."

"Yes sir! Straight away!"

I wrote to Pte Heywood:

Dear George,

I should be glad if you would send the £4 you borrowed for the wedding ring. It was your duty to tell me you were going overseas and to have made arrangements about the repayment. However, please let me have the money immediately.

Hope you soon settle down to life overseas.

A reply came in late November:

Dear Sir,

In reply to your most welcome letter I am sorry I have not written because I haven't had your address until today. About sending the P.O. for the money you lent me, well, I will send your address to my wife and tell her to send it on as soon as possible. Hoping that you are keeping all right. From yours truly, George Heywood.

In December, I wrote to the wife:

Dear Mrs Heywood,

I am sorry to have to write this. I was hoping to have heard from you some time ago. Your husband, Pte George Heywood wrote me and said he had given you my address to forward the £4 he borrowed. It is now almost four months since I lent him the money and he promised to repay it in six weeks. He has made no effort yet, and I should be glad to have the amount as soon as possible.

Yours sincerely, Albert J Ball.

I wrote the letter on Service paper, in official Army format style, with Chaplain's full title Rev Albert J Ball CF, address and file references.

I received a reply in a tatty white envelope.

Dear Albert, i have just received your letter which concerns my husband it came to me as a shock because i didn't know anything about it and George never gave me your address. i was very surprised to hear he had been borrowing money because each time he came home he had what he wanted, you see Albert i haven't been working as i haven't been too well. i don't know what he wanted the money for and never knew anything about it. Anyway i haven't heard from him for five weeks he has been posted but when i get his address i will send it to you then you can write to him to get your £4 back.

Yours sincerely, Lynda Heywood

'Dear Albert!' indeed! Much amused, I corresponded no further. I neither saw nor heard anything more from George or his wife; and I sometimes wonder if the ring was gold or platinum.

* * * * * *

CHAPTER 12

Padre's Hours

The regimental band played in the Ante Room on Regimental Dinner Night, a very formal, traditional occasion. At our CO's express wish they played Gilbert & Sullivan music. All officers were expected to attend and were seated at a long table on which a narrow white tablecloth ran from end-to-end on each side. After the meal when the table is cleared of dishes, a soldier stands at each end, one for each cloth and on the precise signal they give the cloths a quick tug making them slide swiftly along the polished table in opposite directions to be collected smartly by each soldier. As I remember, all officers stand for the ceremony and no officer left the Mess until the Commanding Officer (CO) had first retired.

My Senior Chaplain said that a Padre in his uniform and clerical collar was "a reminder for the men of home and the deeper things of life." True, by my clerical collar and uniform I was representing a man's religion and spiritual matters; but I believed that a chaplain should as far as possible, share the soldier's life. At the 19 Infantry Training Centre I joined the men in the gymnasium, in their games, outdoor training exercises and met them informally around the barracks. I wanted to be helpful, particularly when talk often concerned their lives and problems, hopes and dreams and of course their grumbles and grouses. My CO said, "Padre, if the men stopped grumbling I should think something was *really* wrong."

Church Parades and Padre's Hour were compulsory. But military training was so intense there was little room for many Padre's Hours and I felt my real work was probably more effective on informal occasions than in the obligatory.

There is a splendid social, intellectual and comrade-mix in a conscripted Army. Padre's Hour discussions, with large or small groups of men, provided evidence of various educational standards and backgrounds.

It was quite noticeable on one occasion when I had them prepare a 'Balance sheet of the Church.'

I chalked lines on the blackboard in columns headed DEBIT, CREDIT. Things that they said were wrong with the Church to go on the debit side, and what they thought was good to go on the credit side. I left it for them to say and I chalked up their answers. Starting with what was wrong, there was no hesitation with the first two or three replies, but longer pauses as others were added. When they could think of nothing more I said, "Well, I'm inside the Church and I can think of a lot more." Laughter! "Now, what has the Church done right?"

From one bright lad came the answer immediately, "Education began with the monks in the early church." A short silence and then from another, "Care of the sick! Hospitals."

"Anything else," I asked. Quickly there came from the same bright lad with the first answer, "Care of the insane! Due to the work of... er... Tuke, I think was his name."

The Result

Bad......Wrong	**Good......Right**
1. Bishops' palaces	1. Education - schools
2. Wealthy landowner	2. Hospitals - care of the sick
3. Snobbishness	3. Care of the insane.
4. Unfriendly people	
5. Long sermons	
6. Old fashioned	
7. All old folk	
8. Too much pomp	
9. Pew rents	

One night, I joined a Company on late night training. This time it was under live ammunition and on this exercise, officers wore no badge of rank. It was rigorous.

The men returned to barracks in the early hours, really tired out. Hot cocoa was provided and I joined the queue. A corporal behind the table was serving from a large urn. He served the lad ahead of me. Not to the lad's satisfaction! The mug was barely half-full. He held it out for more.

"That's it, mate. Op it!" The corporal snapped.

"Fill it up!" I said. "Fill mine up too!" The corporal reared up and glared at me fiercely. The man ahead lowered his mug. The corporal told him quickly, roughly: "That's all you're bloody well going to get!"

"Fill it up," I said again.

"What the bloody hell do you think you are doing? You'd better watch it mate! You're in for trouble!" The corporal really laid it on thick.

The young subaltern Duty Officer, standing behind the table, was obviously amused. "That's the Padre you're talking to," he said. The corporal lowered his eyes. Then, a little shamefacedly he said, "Sorry, sir!" He filled both mugs.

"Corporal, you've been indoors making cocoa. These men have been outside training hard," was all I said.

One morning, the Guardroom Sergeant telephoned. "Padre, I've a very distressed man here. They brought him in last night for us to keep an eye on him and he's here banging his head against the wall, asking for the Padre. His pal is the only one who can do anything with him." I saw the boy Max, standing facing the wall; he was calm now. His pal, Keith, had an arm around his shoulder speaking softly; comforting him like a mother would a child. I took them both from the Guardroom; first to the Doc's surgery and then to my office.

On the way, in the middle of the busy parade-ground, regardless of the activity going on Max said, "Padre, I must pray" and immediately got down on his knees. He was quiet for a few minutes.

Sitting by the window in my office, he said, "Padre, cats were running all over my feet in the Guardroom." The next minute he said, "Padre, there are devils in this office." I got up from my desk and went over to him. "Max," I said, "you listen to me! I'm the Padre! There are no devils where the Padre is." For a little time he sat quietly near the stove then he seemed to become distressed and I kept an eye on him. Suddenly he took off his ring and threw it into the hot stove. I felt bad about Max and wished I could think of something to say. I wanted to say, Now, take it easy. Calm down. Why have you done that? Tell me why!

I immediately telephoned the Adjutant making it clear that the lad was not to spend another night in the Guardroom. I then arranged to take him straightway to a Military Hospital. I called for a driver to bring my 15-cwt. truck and set out for York with Max and his pal Keith sitting in the back. Ten minutes later, Max wanted to get out to pray. On a grass verge, he was down on his knees again. Unfortunately, at York they sent us on to Preston, another long journey. There they admitted him to a psychiatric ward. Keith came back with us to Formby and it was after midnight when we arrived. A tiring day!

During treatment, they found the cause of the trouble. Max had fought in Italy and a shrapnel-wound had blinded one eye. Back home on leave when his girl friend saw him thus disfigured she broke off the engagement. Hence, presumably, the ring episode!

With treatment, he recovered normal life and they posted him to light duties in another unit.

Keith went back to his B Company.

I still bear a reminder of my time at 19 ITC Harrington Barracks – a scar which has the appearance of a contused wound. One day we were all ordered to have a vaccination against something or other, I forget what, but what I cannot forget is that the needle was infected and my left arm became swollen to twice its size with blood poisoning. It was in a sling for a long time, very painful and troublesome.

In January, my posting came.

To Headquarters, 61 Division, 16 Broadwater Down, Tunbridge Wells.

******

CHAPTER 13

A Ropey Thing to Do

In the Army, you stay put until you receive a Movement Order.

My Posting came by letter (CRWC No.4/88235) from the Assistant Chaplain General, Western Command. Seven authorities from the Chaplain General downwards, received copies. Consequent upon the letter, my Adjutant No.19 Infantry Training Centre sent me a letter;

'Rev A J Ball, CF... Please arrange to report to Headquarters, 61 Division, 16 Broadwater Down, Tunbridge Wells... Railway Warrant for journey is enclosed.'

I duly reported to HQ Headquarters, 61 Division, 16 Broadwater Down, Tunbridge Wells and was then attached to 2/7 Warwick's Battalion HQ at Godinton House, Ashford, Kent. Like many other country houses, the Army had requisitioned Godinton House and Park. Following the recommended procedure, I reported to the Adjutant; then made sure they had allotted me a place to sleep - the palatial 'Princess Bedroom.'

With the benefit of my Formby experience I quickly settled in and was soon acquainted with Company Commanders and their men. The first time I visited 'C' Company I met Major Gibson, the brother of Guy Gibson, VC, RAF, and arranged with him to have Padre's Hours regularly with his men. He was kindly disposed to the idea and was interested in such details of camp-life that mean so much to the well-being of the soldier.

I went to Hothfield to give some information to a Brigadier regarding procedure for marriage and visited Willesborough Hospital to see some of our 2/7 Warwick's men who were patients. It was an interesting afternoon because one of the Staff Sisters showed me around the operating theatre.

The Kent accent was new to me! I spoke to a 14 year-old boy who said he had been in an argument with a cow. His head was bandaged.

In a farmer's eyes one isn't regarded proficient at milking until the cow has either kicked you or knocked you over. I joked with him about the accident that would make him 'a real milker'. The lad was very amused and later I learned why. When I saw him again I said, "Here's the one who had an argument with a cow!" He laughed. "No Sir, not a cow but a car."

So much for the Kent accent!

The chaplain often serves as the Unit Welfare Officer. In the 2/7 Warwicks were a number of soldiers, tough hardened men who had been a long time fighting in the 14th Army in Burma and were back in the UK on what the Army called 'Python Leave.' We had a sergeant who in India had married an Indian girl who came from a wealthy home with many servants. He brought her to his home in Hulme, Manchester.

A Welfare Association had notified me of the girl's present unhappy plight. The soldier's mother was treating her as a 'skivvy' even making her scrub floors. The girl had no life at all. When I confronted the Sergeant he would accept no responsibility for the girl he had married. He told me she was all right, that she was with his mother who was doing the right thing. The girl was only an Indian.'

No way could we make him see his obligation. I let the man know what I thought about him in language he could understand.

With the co-operation of the Welfare Association and until I could fix a flight to India for her return home, I arranged for the girl to stay with a returned missionary and his wife. The sergeant grudgingly accepted the situation.

Godinton Park was a splendid area for sports. The one and only time I played Rugby was in the match 'Officers versus

Other Ranks.' The Officers were a man short and they persuaded me as the only one available. What position I played I don't know. With what result I don't know. I only remember standing once on the touchline and throwing the ball towards two lines of men.

In the Hall was a massive fireplace about eight to ten feet wide with a log fire always burning. The Doc and I chopped the logs and made the necessary shavings to keep the base aglow for the logs. It was a pleasant occupation in pleasant surroundings, with pleasant conversation.

On one occasion when Dorothy Hall was in London I arranged to meet her for the day. I asked George, my driver, if he were willing to take me. He was very willing!

We went.

Dorothy and I enjoyed the day together! George enjoyed his day. It was late when we returned to Godinton Park where a message awaited me from the Commanding Officer. 'Please report at 0930 hrs. tomorrow.'

Oh dear!

"Padre, that was a ropey thing to do," he said.

I explained the circumstances.

"It was still a ropey thing to do. While you were away, your posting came. To India." He handed me the letter.

Subject: - Posting Overseas.
The Reverend A J Ball (328885) CF 4th Class (Meth) has been selected for duty in India. He should proceed on 14 days embarkation leave with effect from 12 April reporting at the London District Assembly Centre on 20 April at 1500 hrs.

Assistant Chaplain General.
Eastern Command.

Before embarkation leave, medical category to be checked by the MO

Inoculations to be completed. Normal scale tropical kit required.

Baggage allowance 1½ cwts plus 1 cwt ecclesiastical kit.

Leave address and medical certificate should be forwarded to this office early. A copy of the General Instructions for chaplains proceeding overseas has been sent to Mr Ball direct.

I digested the copy of the 'General Instructions for chaplains proceeding overseas' and reported at the London District Assembly Centre on 20 April at 1500hrs.

* * * * * *

A.J.B. in India 1945

Dorothy Hall as "Cleopatra"

As a small boy with my family

With the Epworth League

Gateway of India

Our stay at the raffles Hote

Our “Bungalow”

Anglo Chinese school as ICCS

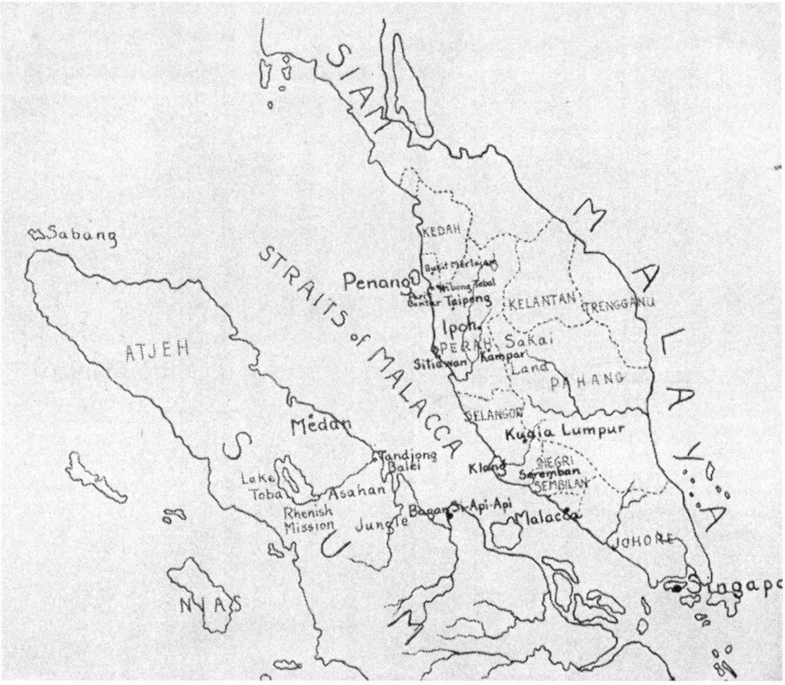

Sketch Map, Malaya

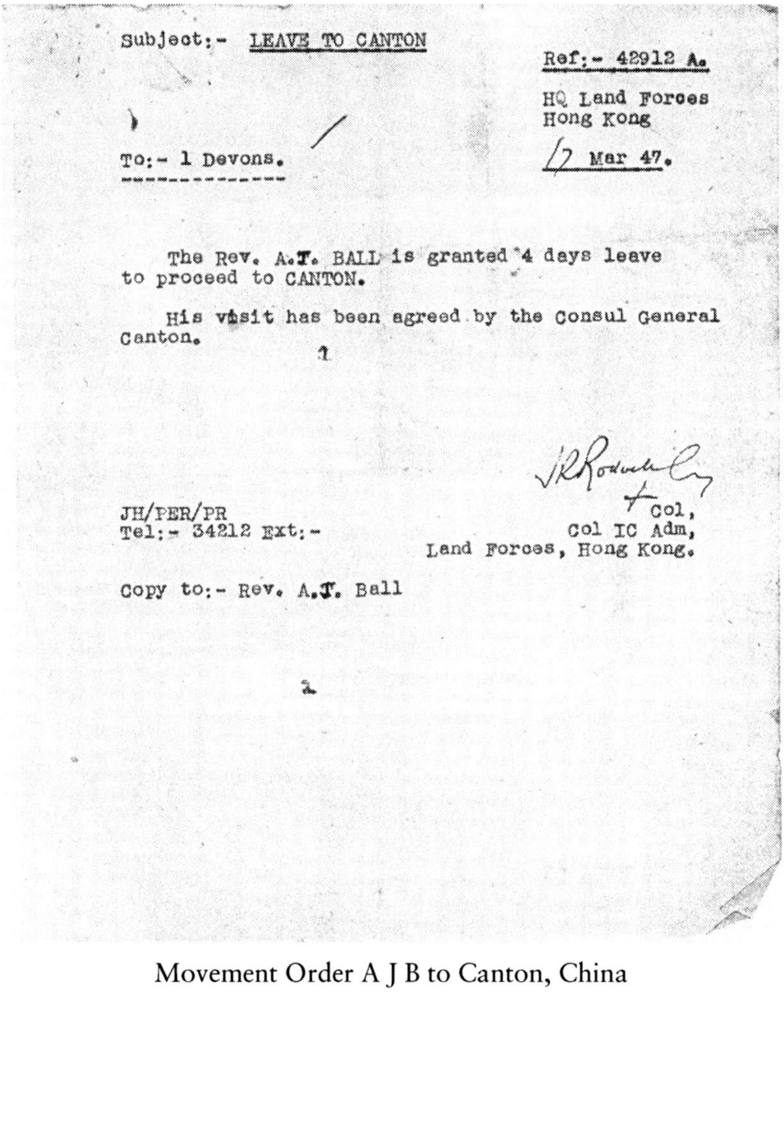

Subject:- LEAVE TO CANTON

Ref:- 42912 A.

HQ Land Forces
Hong Kong

To:- 1 Devons.

17 Mar 47.

The Rev. A.J. BALL is granted 4 days leave to proceed to CANTON.

His visit has been agreed by the Consul General Canton.

JH/PER/PR
Tel:- 34212 Ext:-

Col,
Col IC Adm,
Land Forces, Hong Kong.

Copy to:- Rev. A.J. Ball

Movement Order A J B to Canton, China

19 I.C.C.S., group photograph Penang, Malaya

Military funeral, Hong Kong

Padre's Jeep

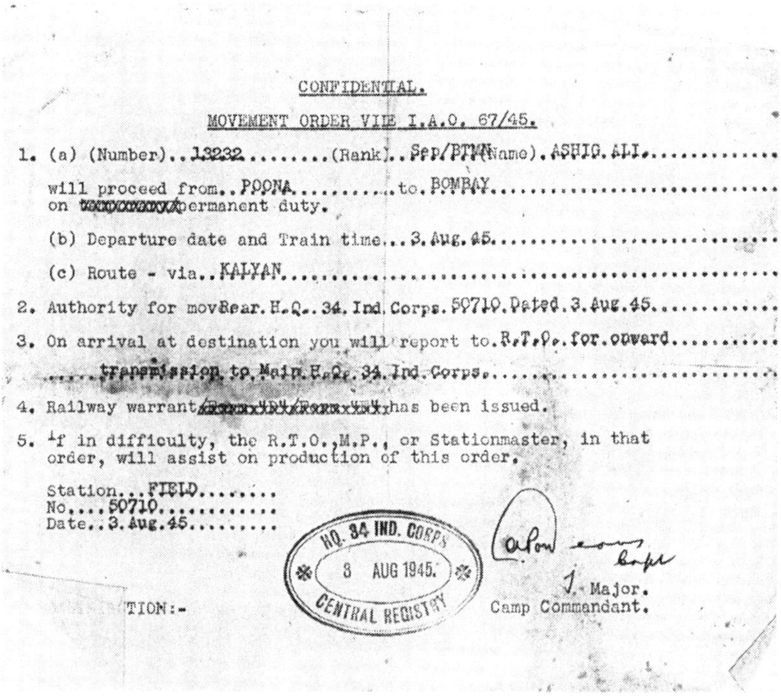

CONFIDENTIAL.

MOVEMENT ORDER VIDE I.A.O. 67/45.

1. (a) (Number)..13232........(Rank)..Sep/BTMN(Name).ASHIG.ALI..............

will proceed from..POONA..........to..BOMBAY..............................
on xxxxxxxxxx/permanent duty.

(b) Departure date and Train time...3.Aug.45..............................

(c) Route - via..KALYAN...

2. Authority for movRear.H.Q..34.Ind.Corps.50710.Dated.3.Aug.45...............

3. On arrival at destination you will report to.R.T.O..for.onward..........
......transmission.to.Main.H.Q..34.Ind.Corps..............................

4. Railway warrant/xxxxxxxxxxxxxxxxxxxx/has been issued.

5. If in difficulty, the R.T.O.,M.P., or Stationmaster, in that order, will assist on production of this order.

Station...FIELD.......
No....50710............
Date..3.Aug.45.........

HQ. 34 IND. CORPS
3 AUG 1945.
CENTRAL REGISTRY

Major.
Camp Commandant.

...TION:-

Ashig Ali's movement Order

My picture of Stanley Viliage 1947

Rope walking at Stanley

Orphanage at Fatshan, Canton

Kowloon, (Goodbye, Hong Kong)

Chapter 14

Poona And Ashig Ali

On May 30th I embarked at the Pier Head, Liverpool, on the *Stratheden* for India. Fortunate to be on such a magnificent P & O vessel, chaplain Paddy Heeney and I shared a cabin with two others. To avoid submarine attack the convoy went far-out into the Atlantic and it was six days before we reached Gibraltar. It was good to stand on open-deck, in brilliant sunshine with a fresh wind blowing, watching other ships in the convoy ploughing their way through endless miles of sea. In the Mediterranean, the order came to change from battle-dress into Khaki Drill Tropical Kit, a welcome change to cool bush-shirts and shorts. In the brilliant sunshine we approached Algiers, which appeared a colourful picture-postcard with tall gleaming-white, red-roofed buildings on the hillside, interspersed with rich green foliage and on the quayside a line of modern buildings with palm trees. Domes and turrets on one large building appeared to be a mosque, until drawing nearer we saw the words 'Casino Municipal.' Traffic and rail-cars trundled along the street. We thought, perhaps mistakenly, that a large number of small white houses hustled together higher on the hillside was the poorer part of the town.

As the ship came alongside the quay, passengers rushing to one side of the deck for the view caused a heavy list; so the alarm-bell was sounded to clear the decks. Everybody back to the cabins! As soon as the ship dropped anchor, decks were crowded again. Down below on the quayside was a crowd of the dirtiest-looking natives, men and boys, clothed in colourful but disreputable rags. One wore a red fez with ragged blue coat and trousers, another had a large battered straw Panama-hat and a bright scarlet apron around his jacket, trousers were at half-mast and their excited rough-and-tumble provided much amusement as cigarettes, sweets and pennies were thrown down to them. The young brown-bodied boys were the most amusing to watch as they caused the Military Police much trouble in cleverly evading every attempt to clear them away from the ship's side. Over on the other side of the ship, a lone native adult was diving for silver coins. He ignored copper.

I preached at the crowded morning service. It was a memorable occasion in such a setting, with windows wide-open to a view of the town. In the afternoon, a regimental band played light music on open deck. At four-thirty we were out at sea again. No-one had been allowed to go ashore, but a large number of French soldiers had embarked. At five o'clock, twelve Salvation Army Officers conducted much-enjoyed community singing and after dinner we listened to Churchill's speech on the radio. Contact with home was the radio news, with the King's VE Day speech and the descriptions of the celebrating crowds in London.

The second service I conducted at sea was at Port Said. The temperature at 90 degrees in the shade and humidity at 84 per cent meant a very sticky heat. We were in the hottest, stickiest part of the voyage.

Near Colombo, Ceylon, we saw a school of dolphins skimming through the waves and leaping, at intervals in unison, clean out of the water. Later, we saw five sharks swimming around. The sea was streaked with yellows, greens and browns as though a paintbrush had been drawn left-to-right, straight across; on the horizon was a line of Prussian blue. That night a full moon and the lighted ships made attractive reflections in the water.

My third service was at Colombo.

On our last day at sea, after three weeks of hot weather it was invigorating to have warm, soft, refreshing rain. It was pre-monsoon period and shortly the monsoon would break.

We disembarked at Bombay. A Senior Chaplain, a Methodist, met us on board and took us to a transit camp where we were billeted for two or three days. On our first day in brilliant sunshine Paddy Heeney and I went into Bombay and discovered some of its wonder - beautiful buildings with lush trees of all colours and sizes lining the roadsides and the balmy air was heavily-laden with the pungent smell of India. In the streets, shops spread out on the pavement with Indians everywhere sitting or squatting, standing or lounging, offering an endless variety of goods, things it had been impossible to get in war-time England. Here was a watch-repairer sitting on the pavement with his tools on a small bench in front of him, there a barber working in a small recess, Indians squatting on the floor everywhere, with baskets full of fresh fruits for sale. Little urchins, beautiful children with dark, chocolate-coloured faces and large brown eyes, oily black hair and lovely white teeth, pestering us continually to buy their wares from trays strapped over their shoulders.

But the shoe-shine boys! So persistent!! As I was walking, one youngster was down at my boots splashing polish with his finger on the already shining toecaps and then looking up with a broad grin on his happy face, said he would make a good job for two annas.

After dinner at the Transit Camp, we went again into the brilliantly-lighted town. Shops were still open and even at that hour vendors were still squatting with their baskets of goods. A smell of lime had predominance. We returned to camp in a gharry, an open horse-drawn carriage, the horse ambling along at its own speed and it seemed in its own direction, through noisy crowded streets and a mass of bodies. Indians were running alongside the gharry and one man with a parakeet perched on his finger jumped onto the step of the moving vehicle thrusting himself and the bird in our faces, pestering us to buy.

All was so new, but bewildering. We were glad to get back to the Cantonment.

We received our postings marked 'Secret.'

Mine was to 34 Indian Corps Rear HQ, Poona. The war in Europe was nearing victory for the Allies but Japan still had to be dealt with. The 34 Indian Corps was part of the Army preparing for the immediate re-occupation of Malaya, which the Nipponese had held for four years.

After a five-hour train-journey from Bombay, Lt Col Penman, DACG (Deputy Assistant Chaplain General) met me at Poona station and took me to HQ at Deccan College. He said I would be his acting staff-chaplain, attached to Corps Signals. My room was one of the so-called 'bungalows' on the college campus, a small semi-detached building furnished with charpoy-bed, wardrobe, chest of drawers and a table.

My batman Teja Singh was a Sikh who could not speak English so we struggled, or at least I did, with Urdu the language I had started to learn on the boat.

On my first Sunday evening, I went to Kirkee, a village about two miles away. The Methodist Church was a lovely building, a garrison church with a large congregation of servicemen and women. Roof-fans were working and all windows were open to the garden. After the service there were refreshments and 'Home Fellowship' where we had a sing-song; and remembered the folk back home. There, I met two Methodist local preachers who were both hoping to candidate for the Methodist Ministry.

Outside, village-life went on in the typical Indian leisurely manner. Heavily-laden bullock-carts ambled along with drivers perched on top calling out continually to their beasts. Women in colourful saris strode gracefully erect with baskets or other loads balanced on their heads. Little children walked hand-in-hand at their sides.

That night, at about 2040 hrs. the sunset was most brilliant. There was no lingering twilight as in the UK and sunlight gave everything on the ground a subdued brownish-pink colour, while exaggerating different hues. The sky was splashed with cloudy reds, purples and greys. It was remarkable! A few officers watching from the Mess-veranda said it was only on rare occasions they saw a sunset like that.

The following Sunday I had arranged for the duty-truck to take me to Church at 1800 hrs. At that hour Teja Singh was trying to make me understand that because he was a Sikh and his religion would not allow him to touch beef, or plates that had held beef', he would not be able to take his work-rota in the Officers' Mess as other batmen did. He brought a note to that effect from his Jhubada. By the time I had sorted that one out it was too late for church, but I went in time for the close of the service to make sure all the men had transport back.

Next day the DACG and I went to Poona where the Bishop of Newcastle, who was spending three weeks in India, held a conference of all chaplains in the area. The notable thing about the afternoon was that for an hour while he was speaking there was heavy rain and thunder.

In the evening, I went to an Indian ENSA concert. More than 600 Indian soldiers were squatting on the floor in three distinct rows, *Sikhs, Ghurkas, and Madrassees.* The orchestra consisted of an instrument, something like a harmonium, plus an Indian beating two small drums with palms and fingers. The Indian dancers were most attractive with their shining tresses of long hair, make-up on their dark faces and colourful saris fastened over their shoulders with gold braid and flashing ornaments.

They danced lithely and gracefully with tinkling-bells attached to their ankles, manipulating arms and hands as though the fingers themselves were doing a ballet dance. Remarkable! Their voices were low and plaintive in a monotonous melody, nevertheless a melody that stuck in the mind. One soloist in this ENSA concert sang a song that was interpreted to me as 'Only God was everlasting and the earth would pass away, the trees, the beautiful ground and we ourselves would pass, but God was always and he would remain.' The audience received this with fervent acclamations and sighs.

On the Saturday afternoon, I went to the incredibly busy, smelly, Kirkee Bazaar, crowded with goats and bullocks lying in the streets! Some places, including Indian restaurants were so bad they were 'Out of Bounds' for the troops.

Throughout the following week it rained incessantly, monsoon rain thundered down. Roads were flooded in parts to a depth of three or four feet, and the nearby river-bed, which a fortnight before had been almost dry, became a fast-flowing torrent. It burst its banks and made a gap in the canal which supplied Poona with water and because of contamination we had no supply for a time; water had to be carried in wagons.

Electricity was failing also, we could barely see to write. But rains, needed for the crops, meant life for India!

After an introductory talk with about 70 men of Corps Signals I was now regularly conducting Padres' Hours. They were compulsory and should be held in the men's training time, not in their spare time. The first was in 'Company Orders' for 0700 hrs. Unfortunately a bad time! Reveille was at 0615 hrs. and at 0700 hrs. the men would otherwise have been occupied in their billets.

A word with the Commanding Officer put that right!

Church Parades were also compulsory; but men told me that what 'got them down' was not the service itself but the lengthy officer's inspection-parade beforehand.

A Scheme was laid on involving the emergency setting-up of rear HQ which meant living at some place or other under canvas. Teja Singh had gone on leave and I now had a batman with initiative; Ashig Ali really was a wonder! He put up a 180 lb tent almost single-handed and directed affairs with great skill.

The trouble was that it rained more or less continually and everywhere became a squelch of mud and grime. Sgt Elgar, the DACG's clerk and I occupied the tent. In spite of the plopping sound of rain on canvas and the discomfort of scorpions, flies and creeping things, we had a fairly good night's sleep.

On the return journey, our convoy made a halt at some isolated spot and almost immediately as though rising from the ground, an Indian appeared with a small child who proffered to do gymnastics to amuse us - for Baksheesh. The contortions into which the child tumbled and fell were weird and wonderful and when he toddled alongside the convoy with outstretched hands appealing for money, few could resist.

Ashig Ali was an experienced batman. He had been a Commanding Officer's batman in the Western Desert and wore the Eighth Army ribbon. I arranged to have him for keeps!

Back in Deccan College, an outstanding event happened. At 1730 hrs. on a hot Saturday afternoon, a soldier came to my open door and called out, "It's taken me some time to find you!"

I recognised the uniform of an army chaplain. Only by the voice did I recognise Ronald Jobling, a Hartley Victoria College friend of the 1938 intake. He had altered considerably; so horribly lank and haggard-looking.

In service in Burma, with front-line troops of the 14th Army down to Rangoon, for three months he had lived continuously on bully-beef and biscuits. Knocked out with paratyphoid, duodenal ulcers and internal bleeding he was flown to a backward area and was on the dangerously-ill list for a fortnight. With his health completely broken, he was medically discharged from the Army and was on his way home via military hospitals. Steadily transferred from place to place since April, he was waiting for a hospital boat to take him home to England in a month's time. We went to the Mess and arranged dinner later.

The Mess Sgt. prepared two boiled eggs (Ronnie was on a diet). Then back to the bungalow where we had a game of chess and exchanged news of college pals – Clifford Sutton, Harry Barnes and others, most of them married now.

At 2100 hrs. I took him back to Poona Military Hospital. We arranged to spend next Saturday afternoon together, perhaps to go to the 'flicks', or the famous Poona races, then to have tea in the Mess before returning to the hospital. Then we could spend the evening playing chess or billiards. I looked forward to that and to further occasions during his time here.

However, it was not to be!

An Indian Casualty Clearing Station (25 ICCS) had been withdrawn from Burma and was waiting in transit at Kurla, near Bombay, to embark for the Malaya invasion and reoccupation.

I had an immediate posting to 25 ICCS
with Ashig Ali my batman.

******

Chapter 15

VJ Day in Bombay

I had everything packed in readiness for the journey to 25 ICCS so that when Ashig Ali reported at 0630 hrs. it would merely be a matter of packing the valise and small kit. At 0720 hrs. he went to his 'lines' in order to report, complete with his kit at 0730 when the duty-truck should be here. The truck arrived at that hour, but no Ashig Ali. Senior Chaplain Major MacDonald, staying temporarily at Rear HQ, was going to Bombay on the 'Deccan Queen' and after waiting five minutes for Ashig, I went to collect him. We returned to the bungalow hoping Ashig Ali would be there. This was at 0750 hrs. The train was due to leave Poona at 0830. If I missed the 'Deccan Queen' I would have to travel with my orderly on the slow 1040 (a five-hour journey compared with two and a quarter).

I asked Major MacDonald how long he would give Ashig before wanting to go. "Two minutes!" was his inconsiderate reply.

We started without Ashig and reached the station at 0803 hrs. The duty-truck returned to HQ. At 0810 hrs. with 20 minutes to spare, Major MacDonald already had his ticket and luggage on the platform "I'm sorry, we could have waited another five minutes," he said. I was too annoyed and disgusted to reply. He knew it!

I telephoned Corps HQ and asked them to send Ashig Ali in a jeep, on the off-chance that he still may be in time for the 'Deccan Queen'. He still had not arrived at 0830 hrs. when the train left, so I had breakfast at the station restaurant and afterwards took a taxi to HQ where I found him waiting with two sepoys for a duty-truck to take them to the station.

I bundled them with all their kit into the taxi and reached the station in good time for the 1030 train; a local, stopping at every station. It was late afternoon when we arrived at Kurla.

Padre Harwood, the C of E Chaplain, already stationed with the 25 ICCS, met us and took us to the Camp some miles away, in a hot and humid basin surrounded by hills. We were living in Nissen Huts and conditions were not good! Bathing facilities were plastic-buckets standing out on ant-infested ground.

We consoled ourselves with the thought that we would probably have worse to face in Malaya. Ashig Ali was an excellent batman and quickly organised things.

From the top of the hill behind the huts, there was a splendid view of Bombay in the distance. Shipping in the harbour could be clearly seen. Looking east, the jungle spread towards the tall mountain Ghats. Padre Harwood and I strolled along a track through the jungle hothouse for an hour, sighting exotic birds and flowers, coming across the odd bullock-cart track here-and-there and occasional clearings which seemed almost artificial. When we accidentally wandered off the track it was awesome. We realised what men of the 14th Army must have suffered in the jungles of Burma.

Two days after our arrival, Ashig Ali failed to appear at reveille.

I reported the matter and they said he was absent from the Roll Call that morning, he had deserted! A deserter? No, that just could not be! A lad of sound character, it was so unlike him to do that. I gave his description for police purposes - 5 feet 4 inches, slim, light brown eyes, dark moustache and a mole on his right cheek.

Instructions were that all packing must be completed in two days time. The rest of the day was spent frantically packing! For the rest of our time we have to live only on what we can carry in our packs.

Our two Padres' trucks arrived - 15-cwt Chevrolets. They were good! Captain Jackson, the surgeon, had to go into

Bombay to collect some medical stores so we went in my truck. After lunch at the Coffee club in Churchgate Road, we drove along Marine Drive to collect the stores. The sea-front was magnificent, so stately and colourful with splendid modern buildings stretching the whole length of the Drive. The warehouse, from which he collected the stores, was in a delightful setting of cocoanut palms and rich vegetation. I offered a small Indian office-boy one rupee to climb and bring down a cocoanut. He brought two and set about stripping them of their large outer fibre-casing. When opened, they were filled to the brim with delicious fresh milk which we drank with difficulty in a bumping truck on our way back to camp.

That Friday evening I was shaving when in the mirror I saw Ashig Ali standing at the open door. "Salaam Sahib" he said as though not a minute had passed since he went away. I had to pinch myself, so to speak, to make sure I was not dreaming. He quietly busied himself with the mosquito-net around my camp-bed as usual. After a few minutes I said, "Well, Ashig Ali - what is it?"

Poor, brave Ashig Ali! He told a pitiful, but manly story. His shirt, wet through with sweat, was torn in places. He showed me his boots - their soles were partly worn away. On the Tuesday night he went to a cinema in Bombay and being new to the camp, its name had slipped his memory. In trying to get back, he lost his way. He then walked 14 miles to the Kalyan Transit Camp, hitchhiked the long way back to Corps HQ in Poona, to find out where we were camped. He must have walked many miles on his journey from Bombay to Poona. He said he had walked 40 and had 60 rupees stolen from him while he was away. He slept the night at HQ. They gave him a Movement Order and a Railway Warrant to come back to me. When his train arrived at Kurla he recognised the station and got off; eventually arriving back in camp. The official Warrant and Movement Order confirmed his story (I still have his Movement Order).

Poor Ashig! His lip quivered and his eyes filled with tears when he showed me his blistered heel. Brave lad! He finished his routine work and came to attention with a smile, "Salaam, Sahib," he said in his usual way, then walked – no, limped away with his confidence and self-respect intact and with the packets of cigarettes I gave him. We were together again. He was not a deserter! Truly loyal! What loyalty! I went to the office with my written report for HQ explaining the situation. They laid no charge against him.

Next day, packing was completed. In the afternoon I went into Bombay with Harwood, Bennett and Jackson. After taking our trunks to the Methodist Church for storage we had tea at the ostentatious Taj Mahal Hotel. From our table we could see the noble structure of the '*Gateway of India*' and the exceptional amount of shipping in the harbour. The important news of course was that Japan may surrender at any hour. Back in camp there was no electricity in the huts so, after dinner at eight it was to bed by nine-thirty. These were lazy days. In the hot, humid encampment 20 miles from the coast, we were doing nothing of any need or consequence.

There was so little happening that it was difficult to find material for letters home. The smallest impressions had to make news - fire-flies lacing the trees after dark, or the snake lurking in the grass a few feet from where one was writing, or the chameleon scorching across the sandy earth, its red-slashed body changing quickly to brownish grey as it scaled the tree-trunk to become a mottled green among the leaves.

There is a palm-encircled lagoon on the Northwest coast of India which I suppose is no different from many other lagoons all over the eastern world.

On Friday afternoon, August 10, 1945, we took the Indian soldiers attached to our Casualty Clearing station to this lagoon for organised sports. It relieved the monotony of lazy days of waiting for embarkation orders. There were fresh fruits and coconut milk in abundance. Sun-browned bodies rode the surf of sturdy breakers, swam or relaxed as the whim took. With its stretch of hot, golden sands it is a familiar Technicolour picture. Yet in reminiscence its enjoyment was for a few British officers, a quiet prelude to a change in world history.

I remember the torrential rain of the evening - a monsoon breaking with thunder and lightning. Most of us went to bed early but the rain on the corrugated roof of the dimly-lit Nissen hut, crunching like the tide's ebb through a shingle beach, kept me awake.

Suddenly, there was a commotion outside and we wondered if a thief had been caught. Then Capt Jackson came yelling through the door the news of Japan's surrender. We were all out of bed quickly. "It's on the wireless," he said.

In the mess, we found a few officers crouched around the radio set. London had been rejoicing for hours. Capt Jackson brought glasses and filled them for a toast. In the light of the hurricane lamp we stood around the table. "To the end of the war!" Then: "To England and the future!"

Five days later, Jackson and I were in Bombay on the night of VJ Day. We walked towards the Taj Mahal Hotel. A 'Victory' tramcar Illuminated by hundreds of coloured bulbs trundled along the street. Floodlights pierced the tracery of delicate arches and slender pillars on a beautiful domed building casting their shadow on the low-lying clouds - a silhouetted palace in the sky.

There was still an exceptional amount of shipping in the harbour.

Searchlights from either side threw long powerful beams on the commemorative '*Gateway of India*' making it a clear-cut black-and-white study.

Rockets pirouetted from the ships in the harbour; green, blue, red and white. Very-lights accompanied the vibrant syncopation of hooting sirens. Behind us the Taj Mahal was in regal mood. Flags were flying and a large letter 'V' shaped itself in a blue neon sign.

Thousands of Indians, mostly men and youths, jostled each other in wild excitement. In their shrieking mouths, chewed betel-nut splashed tongues and teeth a vivid red. Naked children scrambled around our legs to join an ever-growing procession, which trailed five British sailors staggering arm-in-arm singing the glories of England. Under the main arch of '*The Gateway*' the crowd encircled them to a standstill. The tune changed and a rhythmic hand-clapping increased in tempo so that the whole thing became a frenzy of primitive eastern dancing.

We decided to get away from it and made our way through the crowd, passing a group of Muslims herded into a corner of the building prostrate on their prayer mats.

From a line of closely parked cars, a practiced and plaintive "*Baksheesh, Sahib?*" drew attention to a beggar-woman sitting on the running-board of a large American car. The dirty sari covering her head was drawn aside over the shoulders to allow the child in her arms to suckle her naked breast.

The woman raised sightless eyes and her smile revealed a row of broken and decayed teeth. Without turning its face from the meagre comfort of the breast, the child lifted its hand for an expected coin.

We were both glad to get into the cool air-conditioned hotel where our minds stirred into remembrance of the frustration, disappointment, sorrow and success of six years of war.

* * * * *

Chapter 16

A Question of Conscience

The Japanese Emperor had surrendered to the Allies on August 16 but it was not known if the troops in Malaya had laid down their arms so the scheme 'Button', the invasion and reoccupation of Malaya, was to proceed as planned

At Bombay on August 27, the 25 ICCS embarked on the Pacific Steam Navigation Company's ship *Orduna* which in peacetime travelled to Chile and was more than 30 years old. We remained at the dockside until the 29th when we moved out into the harbour to join a large armada of ships, similar to armadas at Madras, Rangoon and other places, ready to sail to Malaya.

About 150 miles north of Singapore we sighted the Malayan coast. The French battleship *Richelieu*, the cruisers *Ceylon* and *Nigeria,* with a number of destroyers were among the hundreds of vessels and small craft forging steadily down the Malaccan Straits, along the mine-swept channel.

One evening after first supper, two ICCS medical officers and I went up on deck. We sat on the flat top of an additional lifeboat, glad to feel the slight breeze caused by the ship's movement. The swift, gliding flight of flying-fishes could be seen only with difficulty in the gathering dusk. The first star could be seen faintly astern and over the western sky lay the yellowish-grey clouds of the tropical sunset. "This is the sea that Conrad describes so often as having a breathing spirit of its own," said Captain Mace, the physician, a fair, thin man with slightly stooping shoulders. "Why Doc! You're quite a mystic," I said.

"God forbid! I'm an Agnostic!"

I laughed. "Does that entitle you to ask God to forbid anything?"

"Strictly speaking, no!" he replied in his slow soft voice. "What do you believe in?" I asked. Mace looked at me under heavy lids with eyes that had a deceptive mildness. "I neither believe nor disbelieve in the existence of God" he said. "By definition I must obviously claim that no one knows whether or not God exists, but I am prepared to investigate both possibilities."

"I should think it's an obvious axiom," I said.

"No doubt you are referring to the fact that since the universe exists axiomatically, it is logical to deduce that someone or something created it; something we call God," said Mace.

Capt. Johnson, the anaesthetist, broke in with "Although it is scarcely conducive in itself to deep philosophy to sit on a stool giving 'snuffs,' anaesthetics to you Padre, one cannot help thinking about and being impressed with the repeated transition from animate to the apparently inanimate. Sometimes I regret to say, even to the really and finally inanimate. It has been claimed that the dividing line between the living cell and the larger molecules of matter of the organic structure chemically, is becoming increasingly difficult to draw. I don't know if that contributes anything to the point at issue." With that, he lapsed into silence.

Mace continued: "The division between the animal and the vegetable kingdoms is not a line. Or if one imagines a line, certain simple organisms lie on it, having characters belonging to both sides. Similarly, as Johnson has said, the protein of the simplest living cells is closely approached by synthetic chemical products which show some of the characters we once took as signifying the presence of life."

"Keep going," said I.

"We all know how light behaves like waves; sometimes obeys the laws governing minute but discrete particles. The prime characteristic of matter called mass, is synonymous in the ultimate analysis with energy, which is a prototype of spiritual force. So the line would appear to be continuous between what you Padre would call the soul of man and a piece of stone lying on a hillside." I asked, "What conclusion would you draw from that?"

"That there is no prima facia case for believing that the spiritual side is anything but a manifestation of what you would call the materialistic side, and at Whitehead might describe as 'a cosmic whole.' Mace paused before continuing. "To turn to the mental sphere, we know of no thought existing without accompanying activity in the physical mass we call the brain. I don't venture to define which is cause and which is effect. If a part of a man's brain is destroyed by an injury or by a growth, he may have disturbance of speech.

"That is obviously a loss of external demonstration of his thought: yet we have no proof that such a man *can* think things when he lacks the necessary part of the brain which would be active if he were a normal person." There was another uninterrupted pause before he continued: "Again, if another part of a man's brain were destroyed his personality would be altered. He'd become boastful, fatuous, short of memory, quarrelsome and perhaps guilty of moral lapses quite out of keeping with his former character."

"What has happened to the soul of that man, Padre?" Johnson intervened.

I replied, "I did notice the use of the word 'accompanying'. The psycho-physical is in parallel lines, with interactions, as you say, but while we can't say with definite evidence that the spiritual governs the material, neither can you say the spiritual is governed entirely by the material."

"Nothing we have said disproves the idea that there might be a soul," said Mace. "The brain might well be a fiddle on which the soul, as a player, performs so as to produce the music - music that is the external evidence of thought."

"Accordingly there may be in our demented man an intact soul trying to play a damaged instrument," I commented.

"We come to the next snag in our search for a soul in man," said Mace, "that of insanity. Insanity is another of those unanswered questions, another argument for agnosticism which is the most logical, but least satisfying of philosophies"

"Surely," said I, "You are forgetting the spiritual forces that lie in everyone's conscience."

"Now there, Padre, you have laid your finger on the only feature that provides any kind of logical basis for a belief in a Higher Power. If one does not assume some outward and mighty direction of human minds, how can one explain the fact that human beings have a drive inside themselves causing them to aspire after good and to cut themselves away from the evil of selfishness?"

"You can't," I said with conviction.

"And what would you say exactly Man did aspire to, and in what way?"

"Truth, Goodness and Beauty, three absolute, intrinsic values in the universe, and eternal," was my prompt reply.

"Very well then: having been led to assume for the present, the existence of a Power other than the mere outward appearances of material things we have taken a very big step. Indeed it is one that leads us far on the journey along which you, Padre, have been led by the teaching and example of your religion." Mace paused and lit a cheroot in a leisurely manner. The discussion continued until it was quite dark.

The swish of the sea against the side of the ship made a soothing accompaniment to the talk. Sitting on the boat in our tropical-drill, the only light cast upon us was from the lantern on the Bridge. Across the dark waters the fairy lights of other ships in the convoy could be seen gliding slowly over the sea as if disembodied. The beauty of the scene was something that could be felt. Nothing could be more fitting to the setting, than a discussion on the spiritual powers that motivated such elemental forces.

The great ship swayed ever so slightly in the scarcely noticeable cross-swell; the bright star behind the mast seemed to sway rhythmically to-and-fro; the Milky Way, that seemed so bright in the equatorial latitudes, formed an archway that rocked gently like a giant cradle for the world.

"It's very encouraging", I said, "that from your detached scientific point of view you come to the conclusion that there is one thing that materialism cannot explain - The conscience of Mankind. That is inspiring!" The soft voice of Mace hardly broke the silence as he said: "That came from the assumption that the conscience of man could not arise naturally. It may well be a development of the social sense which is very strong in all gregarious animals, just as language is derived from the grunts and squeals and the thought from language."

The shape of the old moon had begun to rise over the horizon. At that low altitude, it looked larger than normal as it cast a broken trail of light over the still waters.

"So we don't really know after all," said Mace, very gently.

For the moment the 'Doc' had the last word.

******

5

INDIA AND MALAYA

CHAPTER 17

25 ICCS in Malaya

The '*Orduna*' reached the Malayan coast about 150 miles north of Singapore on Sunday morning September 9 and remained stationed about five miles away from the coast. On Monday evening, at about 1730 hrs. we were literally packed into a small landing-craft which set off towards the shore, to about a mile from land where we waited until 0400 hrs. when a smaller landing-craft came to take us on to the beach. With heavy kit on our shoulders and water up to our thighs, we had to wade 300 yards to land. The sea was quite warm, sheet-lightning made a brilliant effect with the dark trees on land softly silhouetted against the sky. Unlike other wartime invasions, there was no enemy-fire to face. We walked in single file through a wood for about ten minutes and camped there for the remaining hour or two of darkness. We had landed on Morib beach. Fires were lighted to dry our clothes and we ate one of the emergency rations, making tea on a very neat and useful solid-fuel cooker about the size of a cocoa-tin. When dawn broke, as quickly as darkness had fallen with minimum twilight, we found ourselves in a lovely plantation of tall trees and lush vegetation.

I felt it was a promising first-impression of Malaya!

We set off immediately to our Assembly Area about ten miles away. Some walked, but a few of us were able to thumb a lift in a lorry. An amazing amount of material had been off-loaded and the roads, which under British rule were amongst the finest in the world, were crowded with Army vehicles and men. We reached our Assembly Area and waited in a rubber plantation for the rest of the unit. Most of the population seemed to be Chinese, very clean, attractive, and careful of their personal appearance.

The whole population was jubilant to receive us.

It rained heavily in the afternoon for about two hours and again we were soaked to the skin. We billeted ourselves in one of the houses and spent the night in reasonable comfort. The following morning we went on to Klang, 18 miles further north.

Our ICCS troops pitched tents on the recreation ground in front of the Sultan's palace where we cooked a meal and bought fresh fruit, pineapples and bananas for two or three cigarettes! Cigarettes cost the equivalent of nine shillings for three; an egg cost eight dollars Japanese money, equivalent to sixteen shillings.

Most shops were closed. Distribution had broken down but overall, people seemed well nourished. They said they badly needed rice. The Nipponese had done wholesale looting!

Next day at 0600 hrs. we packed and were on the move again; not far, about one and a half miles to an Anglo-Chinese School run by the American Methodist Church. The lovely buildings made an admirable hospital. Beds had already been put in the 'wards' and the whole place was a hub-hub of activity - marquees and tents going up here and there, surgical and medical stores set in place. By night-time our 25 ICCS had received a number of patients.

What little I had seen of Malaya I was thoroughly enjoying. Everywhere was rich vegetation with miles and miles of rubber plantations, banana trees, palm-oil trees, castor-oil plants and cocoanut growing near the roads. Clean-looking houses, some raised from the ground on stilts and many picturesque bungalows were dotted here and there.

The weather at that time was more bearable than the previously experienced Indian weather; cooler mornings and evenings, hot afternoons with some rain every day making vegetation rich and green all the year round.

The only Nipponese we saw were prisoners passing through Klang.

Three nearby bungalows were taken as officers' accommodation. A fourth was delightfully furnished with easy chairs, lamp stands, dressing-tables etc. in preparation for the Nursing Sisters when they arrive. They should be very cosy in such a bungalow.

A few shops were now open but, unlike India with more than plenty, there is little or nothing to buy. During the occupation, the Japanese took most goods; if they saw a wrist-watch on anyone's wrist they would stop the wearer and take it. They looted everything of value. Anything left was safely hidden and had not yet seen the light of day. The one cinema in the town was closed. The American Episcopal Methodist Church was open. Four years ago, before the Japanese stopped it, the Sunday evening English-speaking Service had a congregation of three hundred.

On my second day in Klang the Tamil minister, a smartly-dressed, dapper little man came to my bungalow. "Chaplain," he said, "We wish you to conduct our English Speaking Service next Sunday evening. It will be the first service after four years of Nipponese occupation."

"Willingly," said I. "What time?"

"Five-fifteen."

"Where is your church?"

"Quite close! Just there at the back, over the hill! You'll see it, about half a mile away."

A veranda ran around the back of the bungalow. What he called the 'hill' were narrow gardens on an embankment full of tapioca plants and the occasional banana-tree laden with almost-ripe bananas.

"Tell me more," I said.

"The Nipponese allowed our Tamil services but not English. Four years ago, the Sunday evening English-speaking service had a congregation of about three hundred before it was stopped. But how many will come back?" he sighed.

Unfortunately, on the Sunday evening I was busily engaged at the hospital and arrived five minutes late for the service.

Over 'the hill,' as he called it, leads to the town itself and from the hill-top could be seen the distant blue mountains eastward. The church, a small, clean-looking building in a beautiful setting of fresh green shrubbery and palm trees was just down below, all so bright and picturesque in the brilliant sunshine.

The Tamil minister in a white clerical suit stood waiting outside, anxiously as I thought. "Sorry I'm late," I apologised. "I was kept at the hospital."

"Chaplain, thank you for coming." He was all smiles. "Don't worry! We've altered the time to five-thirty."

* * * * * *

CHAPTER 18

A First Service

When we went into the church, I was slightly taken aback to see only the organist and one young Indian girl present.

A centre aisle led from the Porch-entrance to the communion area where the pulpit stood, on a small raised platform. On the wall behind the pulpit was a simple wooden cross. Overhead, whirling fans hung from the varnished wooden roof and white walls with open windows made it feel pleasantly cool. Outside it was unbearably hot.

Sitting with the minister in the front pew we arranged the Order of Service.

At half-past-five, eight persons were present, including two British soldiers.

At quarter-to-six, with no increased congregation, I said, "Shall we start the service now?"

"Yes! Yes!" The little minister rose quickly. "I will ring the bell." He walked down the aisle to the church entrance. Then came the deafening and direful noise of a bell, hung inside the church, nestling under the porch roof.

"What's all that about?" I asked, when he rejoined me.

"We brought the bell inside. Hid it from the Nipponese or they would have taken it for munitions."

It was a mystery to me how anyone in the small town could have heard that bell; yet people soon began assembling and by six o'clock the church was almost filled - a congregation mainly of young Chinese men and women, some Indians, Malays, Siamese and a few Dutch as well as British soldiers.

I entered the pulpit and conducted the first English-speaking service to be held after four years of Japanese suppression.

The Nipponese had censored the hymnbook. Some hymns were marked with a red-ink rubber-stamp; 'NOT TO BE SUNG.' One hymn I chose to be sung was John Oxenham's

'In Christ there is no East or West,
In him no South or North...'

It was a moving and memorable experience.

Folk were overjoyed that they were now free to worship as they wish, without fear of Japanese Gestapo persecution. One young male member told me how the Japs had once given him the infamous 'water treatment.' Attending the service were the two local ministers, Tamil and Chinese, who had worked hard to keep the church alive despite the many difficulties.

Also in the service was a doctor from Ceylon, who at the time of the occupation was spending a holiday here and was unable to get back home. He now intends to stay.

After the service, the church steward Mr J S Abraham invited me to his home. On the way, he took me to a 'Stationary and Printing' shop belonging to a Chinese church member to see the extent of Japanese looting. There was very little left of stock or machinery. When he learned that my typewriter was in my uniform-case, packed up with my other stuff still in Bombay, the owner kindly loaned me his typewriter. After having biscuits and water, we went on to the steward's home for a musical evening - an Indian family, offering European-style hospitality. Daughter Vicky played the piano and the son played the violin! "We had to hide all English music. We've not been allowed to play anything English for four year, so it's wonderful to hear the English songs played again," said Vicky happily.

For all intents and purposes I became the 'acting substitute American pastor.' The headmaster of the Anglo-Chinese Day School asked me to give weekly scripture lessons to his boys each Monday morning. The instruction I gave was not intensive, because I talked to the whole school of 400 boys at a time and not all the boys were Christians; among them were Hindus, Sikhs, Moslems, and Chinese-Buddhists.

The church caretaker, a slim grey-haired Tamil Indian with a well-kept grey moustache, lived in a little wooden bungalow-structure at the rear of the church compound. His English was not perfect, but he tried hard to make me understand what he wanted, mostly greeting me with a smile and "Good morning! I want..." Then would follow his latest demand, which could be anything from writing paper to tons of earth. I called him 'Mr I Want.'

It did not take long for the young people to restart their Epworth League activities and the Boys' Brigade duly received much-needed uniforms from England. At a regional Epworth League Conference, I met the American bishop Dr J B Amstutz, recently released from a Japanese internment camp in Singapore. When the Japs overran the country he chose not to return to America, as most missionaries had done, but to stay with his people. The choice cost him much physical suffering. That afternoon in the sun-drenched compound, Chinese, Indian, Malay, Dutch, American and English Christians welcomed him and heard him speak of his experiences. I remembered one part particularly when, referring to his decision to stay with his people, he told the story of an American lifeboat called upon to help a vessel in distress during a fierce storm. The crew protested that it was too dangerous to attempt a rescue and futile to launch the boat. The captain's reply was, "We have to go out. We don't have to come back." Years later, on the occasion of the bishop's death I was asked to write of him in the Methodist Recorder and quoted 'Future historians of the church will undoubtedly give him pride of place as a great missionary, Episcopal leader, ecumenical pioneer, theological educator, social worker, inspiring preacher and a beloved pastor.'

I have gone ahead of myself, so back to the 25 ICCS. We soon had nearly 200 patients in the hospital. Padre Harwood and I visited and talked with every patient. One of the officer-patients was Lt Hayes from Corps Signals who had shared my room at Poona, a keen Methodist.

One morning, we walked through the town, a delightfully clean place with some quite new buildings, but there was still nothing to buy in what few shops had opened. Victory-arches had been erected and flags, bunting and Chinese-lanterns were strung up along the streets.

Everywhere we went, lovely little children crowded around us begging sweets, chocolates and especially the biscuits. The poor things had no sweets for four years. One day we found a little Malay child lying in the ditch outside the Officers' Mess bungalow. We lifted him out of the ditch and asked a passing Malay to question what the trouble was – although clearly it was a case of malnutrition. He would be about seven-year-old, but his body was just skin-and-bone. He said he had no home, no parents, no brothers or sisters. He was groaning and pressing his puny hands on his stomach and at intervals his face writhed with pain. He had eaten an army-biscuit and this seemed to have caused the pain. Poor chappie! He said that he went to the local hospital that morning and because he had no letter of authority, they would not admit him. We took him to our CCS and looked after him until he we could get him into the local civilian hospital.

Next day, I spent the afternoon in the theatre watching two operations. An Indian had his chest, shoulders, arms and legs burned with petrol and the surgeon took the burnt skin off. A fact I had not realised, was that their dark colour is only first-skin-deep and his new skin was our colour. The other operation was a leg amputation.

That night there was a marvellous sunset. Seen in a Technicolor film we should have said the colour was ridiculous and unnatural! However, there it was! Unforgettable! Purples, indigo, greens, yellows, reds with little pearly flakes. Tall palm-trees were silhouetted in the middle distance. I had already fallen in love with Malaya. The pace of life was so different; most leisurely! The days were so alike one could easily lose track of what day it was. The scene from our bungalow was hard to describe. I sat on the veranda and typed a letter home. I wrote-

'The sun is shining brilliantly and although there is a light breeze disturbing the palm trees, it is very hot. A gentle slope of rich vegetation covers the embankment at the back of the bungalow. On the road running along the front, at the corner of the lane branching off to Telok Puli is a native bungalow, a white structure, nestling among some very tall, English-looking trees. Tall cocoanut-palms stand out here-and-there and the hedgerows are splashed with vivid red flowers. An occasional jeep flashes by, tearing past the leisurely natives, some on cycles, others walking with baskets in their hands and some beautiful Chinese girls in clean colourful pyjama-type suits with young children dressed in similar fashion following closely at their heels. Beyond, we can see a short stretch of the river, a silver sheet of water with a huge flying boat resting serenely in the middle.'

I showed Ashig Ali a photograph of Dorothy Hall and told him the Memsahib in England had asked how Ashig Ali was and whether he would come to England and work for her.

"Bahut achcha Sahib!" he said. "Torah piche hum England ko aenge. Bahut kam karenga." All of which, if I have it right, means "Very good Sir! Very soon I will go to England and do much work." From which you gather Ashig Ali was still with me.

A member of a Chinese family living in a house about 250 yards away from the bungalow was about to be, or had been, married.

The home had been lighted with oil lamps each night and some were kept burning throughout the day.

Spasmodically, scores of firework-crackers were let off. Almost continuously for five days and nights, a rhythmic drumming accompanied a four-note melody from two or three flutes! It seems that a Chinese custom is for the bride to spend four or five days at the bridegroom's home in celebration and the compliment is reciprocated. A month ago, Captain Ken Brown, the hospital dentist and I were invited to a Christian-

Chinese wedding. Kenneth knew the bridegroom himself a dentist, hence the invitation. The Reception was an interesting affair! The bride and bridegroom, their parents, the best man and bridesmaid sat at a table in the centre of the large hall. All around, at a distance of about three yards from them, were three rows of chairs where the many guests sat. The principals at the table were having a good Chinese meal; guests had only ice-cream and wedding cake. A band, comprising piano accordion, violin and banjo, provided music of the latest songs; some were most appropriate but when the orchestra played 'Jealousy' and 'In the Mood,' Ken and I looked at each other and with some difficulty suppressed our giggles.

I was called upon to make a speech.

One young church member told me about some Hindu marriage customs here in Malaya. Parents arrange marriages for their children, whether or not the young folk love each other. "The girl has to present a dowry to the husband, either in lands, property or money," she said "If the girl is poor she has to give all her few jewels and clothes. Indian women spend a lot of money on jewellery so that if trouble comes, they have their wealth on their person. The prospective husband will first enquire from the girl's neighbours whether she is a good girl and if she can cook. Then he enquires from the parents to confirm this. He then asks how much is the dowry and finally arranges the day when he comes to see the girl he is to marry. On that occasion there is a great feast; the girl has to cook the *Tiffin* to prove her worth." She then told me a long story of her own experience. At the age of twelve, her mother arranged a marriage, but she went into a temper and said she did not want to be married at that age; she wanted to be a doctor. Her mother gave way but when the Nipponese came, she thought it safer for a fourteen-year-old girl to be married; so she tried again. She actually fixed the day for the man, about thirty years old, to visit the home. When the mother told her about the arrangement there was a quarrel and when the man came she refused to cook the meal. When he proposed, she said "I shall not get married! Go away and don't come again!" Mother was angry. At the height of the quarrel the girl said, "You're a widow. Why don't *you* get married again, you're young? Arrange a marriage for yourself, not for me!"

On the mother's third attempt, two years ago, the girl went away to stay with missionaries for a time but on her return, mother wanted to try yet again; there was more quarrelling and this time the mother left home. The girl went to the place where she was staying and told her that if she did not come back, she herself would leave for good and go to Singapore.

Her mother came home. Things were restored to normal and it was then left for the girl to marry whoever and whenever she wished.

The customs are binding upon Hindus and Malays.

She said that in almost every home in the road where she lives, there were one or more young girls who were never allowed out until they are married. When she visits their home, they tell her, "You are lucky to be able to go out yourself whenever you wish."

The fact that the girl was a Christian made the difference.

She was eighteen when the British re-occupied Malaya and throughout the Nipponese occupation she had been working in a Post Office. When I first met her she was back at school hoping some day to become a doctor.

* * * * * *

Chapter 19

Voice of Liberty

During the War, an underground Press published and distributed in the East a pamphlet **'Voice of Liberty.'** I was given the pamphlet announcing the end of the War:-

Voice of Liberty

EXTRA August ***16, 1945***

JAPAN HAS SURRENDERED

(NEW DELHI 16th AUGUST.)

THE WAR IS NOW OVER. JAPAN HAS FULLY ACCEPTED THE ALLIED SURRENDER TERMS. THIS ANNOUNCEMENT OF JAPAN'S SURRENDER WAS MADE JOINTLY BY MOSCOW, CHUNGKING, WASHINGTON AND LONDON. THE NEWS OF THE CONFIRMATION OF THE JAPANESE SURRENDER WAS RECEIVED AT 6.15 MALAYAN TIME THIS MORNING. PRESIDENT TRUMAN HAS INSTRUCTED SECRETARY OF STATE, BYRNES TO ASK THE SWISS LEGATION TO TRANSMIT TO THE JAPANESE GOVERNMENT TO ORDER ALL JAPANESE ARMED FORCES TO CEASE FIRE AND TO LAY DOWN THEIR ARMS.

President Truman in a press conference at Washington told them that everything would only be considered settled when the signature of the Allied Powers of Russia. China, America and Britain had been affixed on the surrender terms together with the Japanese signatories only after this is done can victory day be proclaimed.

The British Prime Minister C.R. Atlee in nationwide broadcast told the British people that Japan today has fully accepted the allied terms and have surrendered unconditionally. The last of our Enemy is now laid low thus the International Fascists have collapsed completely. Atlee went on to say he expressed his thanks to all Dominion and Colonial Forces for their bravery and their stout hearts in living through those days of darkness under the Japanese domination. The Japanese acceptance of the Allied surrender terms was handed to the 4 great powers by Shinegeri Togo through the Swiss legation. Here is what it states:

(1) THE JAPANESE EMPEROR IS FULLY PREPARED TO ACCEPT THE ALLIED POTSDAM SURRENDER TERMS.
(2) THE JAPANESE EMPEROR IS ALSO PREPARED TO AUTHORISE AND ENSURE HIS SIGNATURE BY THE JAPANESE GOVERNMENT & THE IMPERIAL GENERAL HEADQUARTERS, ON THE SURRENDER TERMS NECESSARY TO CARRY OUT THE PROVISIONS OF THE PROVISIONS OF THE POTSDAM DECLARATION.
(3) THE EMPEROR IS PREPARED TO ISSUE HIS IMPERIAL ORDERS TO ALL JAPANESE MILITARY, NAVAL AND AIR AUTHORITIES AND TO ALL THE FORCES UNDER THEIR CONTROL WHEREVER LOCATED TO CEASE FIRE AND TO SURRENDER THEIR ARMS AND TO ISSUE SUCH ORDERS AS THE SUPREME COMMANDER MAY REQUIRE TO GIVE EFFECT TO THE SURRENDER TERMS.

THE UNCONDITIONAL SURRENDER OF JAPAN IS MADE THIS THIRD WEEKOF THE POTSDAM DECLARATION OR ON THE 7TH DAY OF SOVIET RUSSIA'S DECLARATION OF WAR ON JAPAN.

NOW, THE FASCISTS HAVE BEEN TOTALLY ANHIHILATED THE PEACE AND SECURITY OF THE WORLD IS CONFIRMED

AND MARKING (SIC) THE ACHIEVED FREEDOM AND LIBERATION FROM THE FASCIST YOKE.
THESE ARE RESULTED BY THE MERITS OF THE PEOPLE AND THE ARMIES OF SOVIET RUSSIA AS WELL AS THE UNANIMOUS UNITY DISPLAYED BY THE GRAND DEMOCRATIC COUNTRIES OF THE WORLD.
CELEBRATE THE VICTORIOUS CONCLUSION OF THE ANTIFASCIST WAR!

LONG LIVE THE LIBERATION OF THE FAR EASTERN SMALL NATIONS!

******

Chapter 20

An Engagement

The Japanese had used the Methodist Church at Port Swettenham as a cookhouse. With the assistance of the Military, stationed at Port Swettenham, we restored and re-decorated the church there. I conducted the first service after its renewal and many soldiers attended. After the service a young British soldier asked if I would baptise him, as he had never been christened, so I arranged with the steward for the church to be opened next morning; but I arrived to find it locked so I baptised the twenty-year-old in the back of my 15-cwt. Truck.

When the first assault of our invading-troops passed through Klang, one Company camped in the Methodist Church and their vehicles churned up the grounds. I asked the Deputy Assistant Adjutant General (DAAG) at Port Swettenham to loan me a company of Pioneers to put the compound in order and was promised that he would provide the labour and materials for whatever I needed. The Pioneers brought more than 30 tons of earth and gravel to make the compound neat and level. They drained it by putting ditches on three sides and also cut down the straggling palm-trees hiding the beautiful little church

I persuaded the Royal Engineers Works Section to build two wooden gates for the entrance. Until the work was finished I spent from 0800 to 1600 hrs. at the church and felt proud of what was accomplished! When the Malayan Methodist Conference met, what I had done with the Army's willing assistance at Klang was noted and recorded.

One Friday night in November, news came that we were to move some time that weekend and Orders had already been given for the patients to be evacuated. There seemed to be a wild hurry about things! The entire unit had to be packed by Sunday when we expected to go. We felt that having to move so soon after we had settled in Klang was, to put it mildly, 'a bit of a nuisance.' We understood that we were to move 200 miles north to Penang, to take over a complete hospital.

I intended to stay for the Sunday services and to follow on with Padre Harwood.

We actually moved on 10th December, but only as far as the Transit Camp at Port Swettenham.

It was a completely lousy, most unhygienic place, used by the Japanese as an internment camp! Prisoners had plastered the walls with writings and dates. I read one Malay message: 'One year and ten months I stayed in this place – signed M Desa.' Poor fellow!

Nine of our ICCS doctors (who described Army method as organised chaos) were there for eight weeks, doing nothing at all. Conditions did not lead to heights of ecstasy but at least we had a roof over our heads, a bed and food. What more could a man want? And echo answered 'What?'

This was the first Christmas to be celebrated after four years of Japanese occupation and on Christmas Eve members of our Klang Church set off carol singing; the choir in an Army truck and I helped with my Chaplain's jeep. At each house, food, tea and coffee were awaiting us!

Earlier in the day from 0800 hrs. until 1500 hrs. I was at the Law Courts because on the previous Saturday in the town I saw two Indian civilians fighting. With the help of Ashig Ali and two soldiers we managed to separate them. One was wounded and sent to hospital, the other was arrested and I, as witness, had to attend the Court. The case was adjourned until 31st December.

On Boxing Day at 0800 hrs. Lt Hughes and I, together with the Church Secretary, set off in my jeep to Singapore, 260 miles, for business with the Acting Bishop of Malaya. With a break of half-an-hour for lunch and an hour's delay at a ferry river-crossing we made Singapore at 1830 hrs. We spent the next morning with the Bishop and then had lunch on the seventh floor of the Cathay Building, on which the Japanese Flag had previously flown.

Because Lt. Hughes had some luggage to deal with, we spent the rest of the day at the docks where I caught sight of '*S.S. ORDUNA*' the ship that brought us from India to Malaya and since September had done the return trip to England

We saw a Japanese Officer on the beach punishing two Jap prisoners who had been caught stealing and were told that the Officer had already made them run around the buildings for an hour and now, he was hitting them hard in the face. Each time they staggered and fell, he would order them to stand up and putting one leg behind them would punch them back on the floor again. This went on for about five minutes until he was out of breath. I asked Lt Hughes (a doctor) to go to stop it. He said the men were accustomed to such military discipline. Finally, the soldiers had to stand in a traditional manner with their hats on the ground at their feet, while the Officer lectured them. He then ordered them to bow to the British Sergeant Major who was in charge.

On the journey home we stayed overnight at the Rest House, Malacca, a lovely place overlooking the sea. Elsie and Doris Walters, of radio fame, were there at the same time. From the veranda we saw the tall slender palm trees on the islands in the lagoon, shot through with rays of the setting sun. That and the reflection of lights on a placid sea made a wonderful picture.

When I returned to Port Swettenham, it was to find that our entire unit, except for a small rear-party, had left that morning for Tanjan Milam, 80 miles north. Padre Harwood had waited until I returned. Well now, according to HQ it seemed they ought not to have gone! We received later orders, not to move until we were able to go straight to our final destination which from all accounts was to be Penang. The rule is, "always obey the latest order!" We reached the conclusion that HQ had not the slightest idea what they were doing. It all seemed rather silly!

However, for me, the time was redeemed by my continued work at the Klang Methodist Church.

Also at that time, Dorothy Hall and I became engaged.

The Church members organised a party, which they called 'The Chaplain's New Year Party.' Lt. Hughes and a number of our military personnel were there, including Major Blake, the Klang Civil Affairs Officer.

I obtained supplies of foodstuffs from the military for more than 300 children and adults – a whole sack of flour for cakes, 40 lbs rice (for the Indians), two large sacks of biscuits and chocolates and a number of very large tins of fruit. First, there were games, indoor and outdoor, then refreshments and cold drinks – more games, then tea.

The last game of the evening was one in which only those whose names began with the letters A B D H played. The secretary's idea!

Immediately afterwards, he announced my engagement to Dorothy Hall.

Press photographers and reporters were there.

I sent newspaper cuttings to Dorothy in the U.K.

* * * * * *

Chapter 21

Trouble Brewing

Most of our unit was still at Tanjan Mulam while we, the advance party, were here in Ipoh where a thousand Dutch troops were stationed. Our ICCS would be serving their medical and surgical needs, a temporary arrangement until we moved to Penang. My billet was a pleasant bungalow and from the open window I could see, beyond a level stretch of luscious tropical greens and tall cocoanut palms, the blue shape of the highland hills about ten miles away. They looked so close. Early morning was bright with glorious sunshine, the air clear and warm, soft, yet somehow crisp; with the song of birds (until now, something I had missed in Malaya). There was a pleasant feel of England, reminding me of autumn days in North Derbyshire. The tall rubber-trees varied in colour. Some were fresh spring-greens, others were yellow-seared and brown-gold, and still others were like copper-beech; all have slender white trunks with interweaving branches.

From my window, I could see the airdrome. On a sign-board, just down the road were the mileage distances, SINGAPORE 370 miles. LONDON 6,000 miles. Measured as the crow flies, London seemed not so far away, compared with the 8,000 miles by sea. It was an interesting thought that people in New York were geographically nearer than I, to my home in the UK.

Diphtheria seemed to be developing into an epidemic in the Dutch Camp. One of our Dutch patients died. There was a patient in the medical ward for a week, treated for malaria, who did not respond to the treatment. Then the typical spots of smallpox showed themselves. Everyone in the hospital had to be vaccinated.

15 February! The Anniversary of the fall of Singapore! The Nipponese had made the day one for rejoicing and ordered a general holiday in Malaya. Now, this year of liberation, the Communists had intended to force a holiday again, having circulated the shops, warning they must close.

The Military Authorities sent out last-minute notices to the effect that shops must remain open; there must be no holiday, no processions, and no demonstrations. Six spitfires were roaring over the town at 0800 hrs. and kept it up for most of the morning, just in case! The political situation was becoming rather tricky. However, the day passed quietly in Ipoh.

One night an Indian Officer was talking with me about the problem that will arise when the Indian Other Ranks get back to their villages after they are demobbed, having visited different countries and large cities where among the luxuries and attractions they were able to throw off their traditions and customs to mix freely, as for example in this country, with Chinese and Malays (rarely with Indian girls). It would be difficult and sometimes almost impossible for those who came from their dirty little villages and houses to settle down to life with a mere pittance of a few rupees a month to live on. The Officer thought there would be robberies and violence in an attempt to get the money and the luxuries enjoyed in the last few years. Later, a general discussion arose when three Indian officers were confronted with the two alternatives; one - a few more years of British rule until India was united enough to solve her own problems, or two, - for the British to clear out of India giving rise to the risk of Civil War.

The three officers had no hesitation in the choice; "Let Britain clear out now and let's have a Civil War!" When it was pointed out that such a situation would throw them an easy prey to any powerful country, Russia in particular, the Indian Medical Specialist answered, "That would be what a vast number of Indians would wish – they are Communists already. If Civil War came, it would "only mean the death of a few millions, which was nothing!" I learned that this attitude was not uncommon. They did not care what the consequences would be as long as they got rid of the British. The Commanding Officer declared; "Our British troops don't want to stay in India. Ask the average soldier and he will tell you that he wants to get out as soon as he can. India has no attraction for them."

It seemed that some of the Officer-class of the Indian Army had no constructive plans and were pessimistic about the future of their country.

War is the very devil and we are now aware of its consequences!

The situation here was bristling! Trouble brewing! Armed Japanese soldiers were hiding in the jungle around the airfield. A shepherd said that they came out and killed some cattle for food. We are not allowed to travel beyond the town without arms. At the beginning of March there were dramatic happenings in the Ipoh cinemas. At intervals they flashed notices on the screen for troops of the various batteries to report immediately to their units. There was trouble with Chinese bandits in the hills surrounding the town and the troops were trying to clear them out. The Chinese had captured two officers commanding units, and are holding them hostage.

A peculiar incident happened along the Battu Gajja Road. A 3-ton-truck was found in a ditch and the four Indian soldiers with it were drowned. The tragedy was that they were on leave and on their way to a port for embarkation home to India. The MO suggested there might have been foul play.

One night I went to the Odeon cinema to see Clark Gable in 'They met in Bombay.' Pictures of the Armistice Day Remembrance at the London Cenotaph, November 11 1945 were in the news-film.

The film well-depicted the atmosphere of solemnity and remembrance; but the conduct of a few Chinese in the theatre made the showing of the film almost a profanity. At close-up shots of outstanding political personalities, including Churchill, there were noticeable titters and laughter. At the

March-Past of the Women's Services, the sight of grey-haired mothers striding proudly in uniform, as they had the right to do, brought uncontrollable bursts of laughter from different places in the audience. It sickened and disgusted me!

The youth of our generation had a bad name for 'The Victorian Age.'

In a Padre's Hour, we discussed 'Religion in the Victorian Age.' We read an enlightening passage from Arthur Bryant's book 'English Saga.' He wrote; 'This England (last decade England) of the rationalists and the money-makers has no time to consider the England of the Yeomen and the ale-house on the heath. It lost the key to its past and future. Its divided posterity has sought it ever since. The social conditions of that older England were the outcome of centuries of evolution. They left to posterity – the English village and countryside, the parliamentary system, the genius of Shakespeare and Newton, the London of Wren. We have a lot to learn from that community. That character has almost gone.'

It was interesting to note that Bryant recorded the shift of population. 'A hundred years ago it was 15 million (of that, only three and half million lived in London). Now it is forty million (eight million living in London).' In discussion, we were led to see that in spite of the curse of the Industrial Revolution with all its misery, it produced the character that built up the glory and splendour of our English nation and Empire. Glimpses of it could be seen in the epic history of the Dunkirk retreat and the solidarity of the common people with their 'grit'.

The group concluded that the Victorian system of Economics failed to adjust itself to the new Industry mania. Previously our English system was based on the home, individual craftsmanship and Religion.

The majority of that particular group of young men felt we needed to get back to those values!

******

CHAPTER 22

Nursing Sisters Arrive

The headmaster of the Anglo-Chinese School asked me to conduct the religious service for the boys at his School at 0800 hrs. on Monday mornings. The majority of the 250 boys in the chapel were Malays, Chinese, Tamils and Sikhs, with ages ranging from 12 to 20 years. They chose two hymns, 'Holy, holy, holy, Lord God Almighty' and 'O Master, let me walk with thee.' It was a unique experience to hear those boys, Mohammedans, Buddhists, Hindus and Sikhs singing Christian hymns to their hearts content. The Christian influence surrounding them surely must have had some effect, although being a government-aided school it was not allowed to proselytise. At lunchtime, I went to the Anglo-Chinese Girls' school to a Literary Meeting of the girls from High Form; beautiful children in immaculately clean Chinese dresses. What interested me was that every girl had thick, jet-black, shining hair. I talked about the Way of Life of English children. They enjoyed the stories of the wartime evacuees.

An Indian Doctor and I were speakers at a 'Moonlight Camp-Fire' organised for the Geographical Section of the Boys' School, the first meeting of the Society since 1941. About 180 boys were there and when we arrived it was chaos because a few minutes after they had started in the open compound, the rain came and came heavily for an hour. The boys were sheltering under a Japanese-built basha, yet from the yelling and the noise it seemed they were good sports, having great fun. They only had two or three cycle oil-lamps for lighting, but the show went on! The clamour of rain on the roof was a backing to the Chinese, Hindustani, and Malay musical items.

The Ipoh Epworth League held a 'One Day Institute' on a Friday and Saturday in February. I obtained permission for 20 Katies of sugar, 75 Katies rice and 15 tins of milk to be bought at controlled prices, total $14 whereas in the Black Market the rice would have cost anything from $50 and the milk at $1 per tin. I also arranged army transport for the Sitiawan group 60 miles away.

Major Kenneford and his surgical team joined us in Ipoh. They had stayed behind at the Klang Hospital to rejoin us when we reached Penang, but the order for us to move came earlier than expected - to Ipoh. He shared my room! At bedtime, we were in conversation until 0230 hrs. talking about religion: "It depends what is meant by faith," he said. "I can never quite understand it. What do *you* mean when you talk of faith in God?"

How could I best explain what faith meant to me? It had cradled me, suckled me, reared me, even forsaken me but I had groped until I found it again, although my plea was ever, 'Lord, I believe; help Thou mine unbelief.'

"Faith for me," I said at last, "is a sense that God is real, that he has knowledge of every one of us, that he takes a guiding interest in our lives, that we are responsible before God and must place our trust in Him."

"Then strictly speaking, Padre, I haven't any faith. That's a step I can't take. I believe in some sort of a God but I can't believe what Christianity says about Christ and God." I breathed a swift prayer for help and then began; "Either there is a God or there isn't. If God exists, it's reasonable to think we have some relationship with him..."

"Go ahead, Padre."

"Believing he is real, men and women have reached out spiritually into the unknown and found by experience that he is there..." I struggled for an analogy. "Like a baby in a cot putting out a hand in the dark to the mother he believes to be near and finds his hand taken in hers." There was another long pause. Finally, he spoke and his tone was slightly bitter. "What would you say if the position were reversed? The mother put her hand to the cot and there is no baby?"

"This concerns you personally?"

"It does," he said quietly. I was annoyed with myself for having chosen such an analogy. I had known little of Major Kenneford's private life. He showed me a photograph of a lovely little boy. "He was killed in the Liverpool blitz."

Soon he was telling of his wife's embitterment at the death of their baby son; of a relationship that became so strained as to make life together impossible; of letters they had written to each other since they had parted, letters that brought no reassurance. "You're both young," I said. "There's time yet."

"My wife can't have another child, Padre." The words had stinging finality.

I tried to understand his feelings; the loss, frustration and despair. But how could I share the man's darkness? What mattered most was for God to become so real to him that the Divine presence would lighten the dark valley. "God doesn't intend you to become bitter," I said. "Put your hand out to Him. You'll find Him there." But words seemed futile!

** ** ** **

There was a buzz of excitement in the officers' mess as the Commanding Officer announced that a contingent of Nursing Sisters would join the unit on the following Tuesday. Until now, the staff had consisted only of males. "I suggest we might give them a bit of a slap-up meal," the CO continued. "After all, we must give them a proper welcome. How about it?"

"A twelve-course Chinese meal," suggested an enthusiastic Lieutenant.

"Right," said the CO immediately. "I take it we all agree to share expenses." The men readily agreed.

Work at the hospital was exciting enough, more so because in addition to medical and surgical it included neurosurgical and psychiatric treatment. However, some female company would certainly be welcome.

The CO booked a Chinese Restaurant for all of us. It was to be a twelve-course meal. At 2000 hrs. on Tuesday we arrived and sat at tables where chop-sticks and a set of soup-dishes were laid out for our use. Two Chinese instrumentalists provided music. First, the waiters none of whom spoke English, brought China-tea in a handle-less cup, then they brought a dish of delicately perfumed hot-towels which after use were collected and taken away.

Then the meal started properly with a large bowl of soup placed in the centre of the table for everyone to help themselves.

Some of the dishes that followed I neither can remember nor describe, but I know there was chicken, jellyfish and starfish, shark-fin soup, bird-nest soup, soups with frog.

So, the meal proceeded. Trying to eat with chop-sticks caused much fun!

Iced blancmange and jelly, with a cup of tea finally rounded it off.

After the meal, the CO took us to the Celestial Cabaret - a dance hall in Ipoh.

Back at the bungalow, I had a dose of Enos!

******

Chapter 23

Penang

PENANG Island is a luxurious gift of nature. The Americans call it '*The Pearl of the East.*' We were stationed in Glugor (in what I understand is now the University campus) the building was reasonably suitable for a hospital. We were billeted in three large detached houses - so-called 'bungalows'. Looking east from our bungalow one caught glimpses of the sea and the mainland-hills beyond. A two-minute walk along a pathway, through a glade towards the beach, brought us to a cute little open-air swimming-pool set in a secluded valley surrounded by palm trees and rich shrubbery; all in the hospital grounds.

Back to my story; on April 1 Civil Affairs took over from the Military Administration and many rumours were flying around. A hospital patient, the Sub Area Commander, told me that Sub Area Penang would close down in June and by September five out of six troops in Malaya would have gone. Georgetown was comparatively quiet in an evening, deserted of soldiers. Most of the troops on Penang Island had already left. We thought all this meant that our 25 ICCS would soon not be needed. The Admin Commander made a wild statement. He said, "Within ten days or a fortnight the CCS will close down." I could not see that happening! However, it seemed that in a few months we should have to disband; for rumour had it that in December there would be a general demobilisation. Nevertheless, work continued.

We had a team of twenty-eight doctors, British and Indian. Surgeons, general medical doctors, a neurosurgeon, psychiatrist, radiologist, dentist, Nursing Sisters, a Red Cross social-worker and of course importantly, ward-orderlies and ancillaries, mostly Indian Other Ranks.

A week after our arrival, I conducted my first service in our little chapel; a simple arrangement; the altar was dark-stained wood with an embossed cross of lighter-coloured wood on the front panel. A blue cloth behind the altar had a gold cross worked into it. Electricians had fixed wall-lights on either side and on the left side I had a kneeling-stool and a small table with a crucifix for the Roman Catholic Padre.

Matron provided a small cross and a vase of flowers for the altar. When the Principal Matron of SEAC (South East Asia Command) visited the chapel with our Matron, she really enthused.

On Palm Sunday, we had Holy Communion at 0800 hrs. One of the Nursing Sisters also attended. The morning service was at 1000 hrs.

In the afternoon I visited every patient. In the evening I preached for the first time in the Georgetown Methodist Church, a beautiful church with a large congregation of mostly young folk in their early twenties! The choir was in place for the first time; the girls dressed in white, each girl wearing a red rose. A few of our soldiers had also joined the choir. It was a memorable service, unique because two American missionaries, who had come back to Malaya, were in the congregation and received a glad welcome. Also, two Chinese children, about three years old, were baptised. The stewards provided refreshments for army personnel after the service.

Next morning, about a hundred young folk were going on a picnic; a whole day affair from 0800 hrs. I helped to transport them with my 15-cwt. truck and had the day with them. Two bus-loads left the church and we spent the morning bathing at the chosen beach. A large bungalow was at our disposal for breakfast and lunch.

The neighbouring bungalow was the 'St. Andrews Leave Camp' and a number of the British Service men staying there joined in our fun and games. The day was hot, the sea pleasantly warm, but in the afternoon it became rather rough. At six o'clock, we had our devotional service on the beach.

When we returned to Georgetown Mr Khoo, the Chinese assistant-pastor, invited me to meet the two returned American missionaries and have supper with them. Chinese soups are remarkable! (No Bird's Nest soup this time!) Heat rising through a funnel from a charcoal fire underneath a large pot on the table kept the soup simmering hot. They put in an assortment of fish, fowl and vegetables and the result was delicious! I left at 2200 hrs. taking some of the guests home in my truck and so back to the CCS.

The following Thursday, Lt Nash and I called at the Wireless and Cable Office where the mechanics of sending a cable were explained to us; dots and dashes of the Morse-code came out on tape as a mark below and a mark above the centre line. At that moment two were being sent to Singapore, two to Madras and one to Colombo. We watched as a message from Singapore was received simultaneously here and at Alexandria. The Officer had been in the job 35 years and was as keen as ever. He said it needs only three minutes to send a cable to London and early in Septembe he was the one to send the first cable out of Malaya for four years.

Later that day I had a pleasing visit from the Roman Catholic Padre and we arranged to have a day or two exploring the island together.

In hospital, a British soldier suffering from Infantile paralysis affecting his diaphragm found it almost impossible to breathe. The docs said they were helpless with this disease and could do nothing about it other than with the use of an iron-lung. Unless an iron-lung was obtained the lad could live only another few hours. The lung at the civil hospital was in need of repair so the doctor telephoned the Army Chief Electrical Engineer and told him to get on with the job straightaway. Poor lad! This had happened just when he was due to go home to be demobbed.

The repaired iron-lung arrived at 0800 hrs. next morning and as the lung does the breathing it gave the lad a chance to fight for his life. Now, he may recover, but no-one could tell.

He was much more at ease but very worried about his wife Maggie and his child John, whom he had not yet seen. He asked me to pray for Maggie and John.

Next day in the VD ward, I met a well-tanned fresh-looking lad with a pleasant smile and a roguish twinkle in his eyes. "Where's your home?" I asked. "I come from Sheffield near the Infirmary where all the rough guys live."

"Are you a rough guy?"

"Not now," was his laughing reply.

"What was your job before you came into the Army?"

He said with another smile, "I came straight into the Army from Borstal. The pal I came in with is already demobbed." Something was amusing him. "Well, what is it?" I prompted. "Well, he was a rags-and-tatters merchant working the streets. He had a handcart and earned just enough for his beer." He laughed "But he's not going to be a rags-and-tatters man anymore."

We talked of Sheffield and its tough guys. I told him I had worked at the Victoria Hall Mission in Sheffield. "Oh yes, I know it, in Norfolk Street," he said. "I used to go drinking in Hayes Wine Merchant next to it on the right side."

"You mean on the wrong side, eh pal?"

Must talk with that lad again, I said to myself.

In the Officers' Ward was an RASC Captain who had contracted VD in Ipoh ten days before. He was a Scot, happily married with a family. His first sexual lapse! "No bloody excuse," he said. His problem was 'the home front.' Should he tell his wife at any time? We talked about the Scottish hills, the Lake District, Wales, and Derbyshire for five or ten minutes before we came to grips.

That evening I went with Padre Oates to Bukit Metajim to a Chinese dinner at the home of the Methodist Pastor, a farewell dinner to eight Australian women Red Cross workers. One was interested in pottery and fired casts and vases in a small kiln in her house, but she said she was more interested in modelling; particularly Chinese heads. Sarah, another very pleasant and jovial young girl, intended to go to England for a holiday to find a friend with whom she could go cycling. The dinner was excellent; many courses including turkey, roast potatoes and green peas. A rather different Chinese meal from the one we gave the Nursing Sisters in Ipoh when they arrived at the ICCS. (Perhaps I am putting too much emphasis on gastronomic in my story, but meals and conviviality have a predominant place with the Chinese.) We missed the 9.30 ferry and had to wait for the 10.30.

At 0230 hrs. I was awakened by an Indian orderly with a message from the surgeon; "L A C Blakely on the DIL (Dangerously Ill List)." I dressed and went across immediately. The RC Padre and I were with him when he died that morning at 1015 hrs. The doctors had put up a good fight for his life.

** ** ** **

When Major Anjaria, Second-in-Command (2 IC), told me that because three officers had recently been coming in so late for dinner that the CO had ordered it to be a **parade** at 2000 hrs. and had set out times for all meals, my first words were, "Well they've asked for it, but I object to a parade every night."

Overall however, dinner became a much more pleasant affair. Capt O'Conner, who is going home in the next few days, handed over the Officers Canteen job to me.

Our unit had still not moved to the Penang Civil Hospital, but the first step in its disbanding had been taken

The British Commanding Officer received a posting-order to Ceylon and in his place we should have an Indian Colonel who would eventually take the unit back to India.

The sooner this happens the better! For one thing, since the staff were changing quickly, it was somehow not nearly the same happy unit as in Ipoh and Klang and had we stayed there much longer, little of the stores would have been left because there was a great deal of thieving.

I regularly visited the Guard Room, a pastoral duty. One day I saw a Chinese girl sitting on the doorstep. "What is she doing here?" I asked the sergeant in charge. "Oh, her? We have a Chinese who was court-marshalled for stealing army blankets. That's one of his wives. He's got three. They take it in turns to sit here most of the day. One brings her baby. It's OK Padre, they're no bother."

The young court-marshalled Chinese orderly explained to me; "I have three wives, Padre! Can't afford three wives on Army pay! I have to do something. Before this I had good luck finding things. This time, I have bad luck! So, I'm here."

One night a large amount of tentage was stolen. A 3-ton truck must have been used and a number of Indian soldiers involved. Troops were confined to barracks for a week. Next night two pitched tents were taken and hundreds of dollars stolen. The radiologist, who lived in the next bungalow, told me that last week his Indian batman stole all his kit, blankets and civvies suit, everything gone. He absconded. Absent-without-leave and a deserter! "But he left his Army Pay Book; so I suppose he's in a village somewhere making himself at home with a Malay or Indian wife!"

Some Indians are prone to stealing, but the exceptional skill of the Chinese was acclaimed common knowledge. They were clever!

They could steal the sheet from under a sleeping-man and not disturb him. It was said they would roll up half the sheet to the man's side, gently tickle him or do something to cause him to turn over without waking and then roll up the other half. Then get away quickly, quietly!

The senior chaplain HQ 7 Ind Div, SEAC had asked me to be responsible for a definite area on the mainland, for units as far north as Sungai Patani and South as far as Parit Buntar, with the occasional visit to Alor Star.

One time, I had been to an outlying Signals Section in Sungai Patani and it was late at night when I returned.

At the bungalow I was surprised to see a white-faced Ken Brown, the dentist who shared the bungalow, standing at the door in his pyjamas with his uniform jacket slung over his shoulder.

"What is it? What's the trouble?" I asked as I jumped down from the jeep.

"A thief just escaped! Chinese! You might have seen him."

"What do you mean? Come in! Tell me about it. You look shell-shocked. We'll brew a cup of tea."

"I was in bed under my mosquito-net reading with the light on! This young fellow came in through the door and he knew I was awake. We stared at each other as he still came towards me.

"While I was struggling to get out from under the wretched mosquito-net he grabbed my coat from the chair-back and ran off. My wallet was in it too."

"But you've still got your coat!"

"I was soon after the blighter! He must have taken fright because he dropped the jacket in the hall, wallet still in it. Only just happened Padre! It's a wonder you didn't see the blighter. I tell you, it was scary the way he was watching me."

"Where was Major Kenneford? Didn't he hear anything?"

"He's gone away for the weekend."

I went into the kitchen and brewed tea. In Ken's room, we drank mugs of tea, laced with Carnation Milk.

'Tea, the Englishman's panacea of all ills and misfortunes!'

* * * * * *

Chapter 24

'The Pearl of the East'

I took three days off and as arranged with John Keegan, the Roman Catholic Padre, we made a tour of Penang Island, '*The Pearl of the East.*' On the coast- road going south we had glimpses of the sea, with smaller islands rising offshore about two miles away. At a little Malayan village on the south-east tip of the island we discovered a magnificent lagoon and although I had only three exposures left in my camera the photograph was justified. Eight boys were sitting on a long narrow-boat on a sandy beach sloping upwards to a row of tall cocoanut palms, which stretched in perspective around the lagoon to the distant blue hills. That and the curve of sand at the water's edge, made a pleasing, colourful picture. I also took a photograph of John sitting on the edge of the boat, talking with the boys.

Continuing, we took a road leading through a hill-pass and arrived at the 'Twentieth Milestone.' (It is 46 miles around the island.) Here we caught sight of a church steeple, so we made our way to what proved to be a convent school. Eight Sisters were sitting at a table in the compound and Reverend Mother made us very welcome. She was an aged French woman, having spent 48 years in Penang. We suggested eating the food we had brought at a table in the large porch, but when Reverend Mother saw the sandwiches she insisted upon our having hot food and soon provided four fried eggs, followed by Chinese food and bananas. Afterwards she conducted us around the beautiful garden. Impressions of splendour, stillness, and sacredness! One tree had showered a bed of scarlet petals on the floor; another was laden with purple flowers and banana-trees were heavy with fruit. She explained that from the large, maroon banana-flower, one petal curls up and drops each day. There were plenty of pineapple-shrubs with ripe golden fruit under large leaves, arrowroot plants with their delicate little pod-flowers, a cocoa-tree with its large pods. With a long stick she brought down one of the pods and on opening it we saw the beans clustered in a soft, pulpy flesh, sweet to the taste, but much unlike the taste of cocoa. The bean itself was the size of a damson-stone. It has to be dried and then ground, like coffee.

The Sisters cultivate the vegetable garden and fruit trees. Turkey-goblins, ducks, fowl, rabbits, a guinea pig and a piggery comprise the farmyard section of the compound.

In the church, we saw fine vestments of rich, beautiful embroidery on Chinese-silk, worked in China!

The road from Balik Pulan led up into the hills, narrow and tortuous like a scenic railway. In a small village we came quite unexpectedly upon a roadside Chinese Opera in progress. Chinese and Malays stood watching the actors dressed in elaborate costumes on a surprisingly well-equipped stage. Ten minutes of that and we continued our journey. Rocks, waterfalls, jungle, and small ravines, with a drop of 100 feet or more from the ever-winding road, made it an interesting but giddy progress. From the occasional clearing there were surprising and splendid views. Far below, a belt of jungle with tall trees of varied colour looked like a patterned carpet with the sea a blue border. One view after another followed in breathtaking succession. Battu Kechil, a 300 feet hill, dropped sheer into the sea. Finally, back in Georgetown we called at the Waterfall Gardens, a paradise garden, making a delightful conclusion of the day. *Such beauty should always be shared!* I thought.

On the Friday afternoon, we arranged to go to Penang Hill on the 2.30 Fernacular Train but we arrived at the station too late. As there was no other train that day we decided to visit the Chinese Temple at Ayer Itam, situated at the foot of the hill. Buildings and grounds cover an extensive area and a guide showed us around. There are gardens with pools for the

Chinese sacred fish and the numerous hundreds-of-years-old sacred tortoises; visitors may buy bunches of special food to feed them. The pagoda is a magnificent landmark. Terraced steps led to the entrance of the Pagoda, flanked on both sides by buildings with pillared porticos and roofs that are perfections of Chinese architecture, with curved, uprising corners and colourful decoration. At its base, the Pagoda is equiangular and rises with seven such equiangular floors of diminishing width; then continues with three more circular floors to the shapely dome at the top. On the minaret, two bells tinkle in the breeze - soft, lulling, temple-bells! In various rooms there were queer symbolic features surrounding many idols and a large Buddha. In one room, a little solid gold Buddha, about four inches high, was behind a small locked iron gate.

A climb of the seven stories of the dome rewarded us with another remarkable, breath-taking view.

We eventually went on the deferred Penang Hill trip.

The train climbs 2,300 feet with a gradient at times of one-in-two and takes twenty-five minutes. It works on a cable system, one train ascends as the other descends and they pass at a loop in the middle of the track. There is a halfway station where it is necessary to change into another train for the remaining, steeper climb to the top. Sitting in the lower compartment as the train ascends, provides a thrilling view of the harbour and the mainland. From the top of the hill, the harbour below is like a tiny model. Ships and liners appear as matchsticks on a sheet of coloured glass and the island itself looks like a coloured plastercine model, similar to the ones used in schools for geographical purposes, showing contours and the like. The southern coast of the island was so clear it seemed only a mile-or-two away. A vast stretch of mainland was visible and the whole looks like a photograph taken from the air. Lovely! Breathtaking!

Certainly, the government did itself credit in lavishly making the hill such a splendid health resort. Charming houses and gardens were dotted here and there; the roses and dahlias would make many gardeners envious.

A most beautiful holiday resort with walks of country scenery and a clean layout of gardens with up-to-date buildings. Such was Penang Hill. John, who had travelled the world over, said he had never seen anything like it.

The Crag Hotel is world famous. We were on our way to the hotel when it started to rain and by the time we reached it, a heavy mist prevented us seeing more than 70 yards ahead. Previously, when the view was clear, we could see small puffs of white cloud floating below us. It was an eerie sensation being high up in the clouds. Now, soaked to the skin, we decided to get back to the station in good time to catch the last train down at 5.45 p.m. I really felt unpleasantly cold! There had been a drop in temperature of five degrees. At the top of the hill, it is normally ten degrees cooler than at sea level. It was 71° yesterday at the summit and 81° in the town. We were very glad to get into the warm cab of the truck parked at the station.

Next day we visited the Chinese caves near Ipoh inside which, temples had been built. Huge mountainous rocks overpower the very pigmy-looking buildings. A large cavern encloses the temple-shrines and as we entered, a very old Chinese priest was reading prayers at the image of Buddha.

A long dark tunnel led into a broad, open clearing surrounded by rocks one hundred and more feet high, out of which trees and shrubbery had sprouted.

At the far end of the clearing was a large empty bungalow with garden terraces and fishponds where previously the nuns had lived. The Japanese had used the place as an ammunition dump. It was interesting to see the 'worshippers' in the Temple burning their sandalwood-sticks beneath the images, trying to find out if they had good luck. They did this by a kind of lottery-game, which was shaking a tin containing lettered-sticks before the 'altar' and the stick that dropped out corresponded to a printed sheet to be taken to the priest, who consults the 'ancient book of words' and tells their fortune.

"I'm going to find out my luck," said John. He came back with his 'fortune' translated from the Chinese by an interested English-speaking bystander -

'YOU WILL HAVE GOOD HEALTH!
YOU WILL LIVE LONG LIFE!
YOU WILL HAVE NO SUCCESS!'

* * * * * *

Chapter 25

Curry and Concrete

I received a signal from ALFSEA (Allied Land Forces South East Asia) instructing me to go to Singapore for a Selection Committee, June 17-20.

Whether I was to be a member of the Committee or a candidate for selection, it did not say. What I did know was that the next afternoon I had to set out with my driver in my 15-cwt truck to Singapore - a matter of 500 miles or more. We set off at 1730 hrs. on the Thursday and reached Ipoh by 2145 hrs. where we stayed the night. Next morning we went on to Malacca, where we also stayed the night. Next day we arrived at Singapore at 1500 hrs. after having travelled 540 miles. I drove 450 of them. Singapore where all nationalities are to be found is a fascinating place, but the cost of living was fantastically high: 'Average sixteen times higher than in England just now,' an MP was reported to have said in the Commons.

Two hours fumbling around Singapore for instructions, first at the RTO; then on to the Chaplain's Centre, which took me quite some time to find; then to the Methodist Church where I stayed the night at the American missionary's manse.

The Selection Committee began work the next day to examine candidates for the Methodist Ministry. Four Methodist Padres were there; one flown-in from Rangoon. When the Committee had finished, Padre Foy (Airborne) and I hired a Trishaw, a pedal-cycle 'taxi,' to take us back to The Raffles Hotel where he occupied the next room to me. We paid the Chinese driver generously but he seemed in no hurry to get pedalling. He spoke very good English. We asked him about his education; "Which school did you go to?"

"It made no difference," he replied. "There are four thousand trishaw drivers in Singapore. Only about two hundred of them are educated. Here am I in the same profession."

"What did you do before?"

"I was a Bank-clerk for seventeen years! When the Japanese came to Singapore I was without a job."

"What happened after they left?"

"Last September I went back to the Bank. They paid me the same rate as pre-war. I have six children and my one-room-house costs twelve dollars; a meal *now* costs five dollars. I couldn't live on that salary."

He went on to say that in six months, he had sold all his goods to provide food and clothing, then he resigned his job at the bank and took up this cycling job.

"It's slowly killing me," he said. "There are hundreds of men in similar position, working long hours. I work long enough to earn ten or twelve dollars a day. When I'm really tired I need to have a rest in the afternoon." The heat of Singapore is always around ninety in the shade, but the humidity causes the Trishaw driver to expend nearly double the amount of energy than what he would need in a cooler climate. "I have to work hard. But I'm better off than the Rickshaw-boy. I do sit on a saddle comfortably for the hard work," he said.

Comparatively, the Trishaw man does have a far easier life than before they turned a two-wheel Rickshaw into a Trishaw, a three-wheel bike. Driven from the side, the front, or from the rear of the passenger, it certainly was an improvement for the man to sit on a saddle for the hard work. The Rickshaw-boy had to trudge between two shafts toiling in the heat, often barefoot, dragging the apparently happy passenger or passengers sitting behind him. The life of a Rickshaw-boy was short; he was literally a skinny human being. Tuberculosis rate was high. To earn anything worthwhile he had to be out early and back home late, often at six in the morning until midnight! Although some Chinese steal to get things easily, I believed the Chinese generally, have patience and tenacity at the root of their character and are prepared to work long and hard for the things they want.

Three weeks ago, my regular driver Natti Singh was demobbed.

"It's a soft job, sir," said Pte Tonkins, a patient in the Medical Ward, when I told him that I had no driver. "*It's the softest job in the army*. One I'd like best."

Natti Singh had been a treasure, a good-humoured, reliable little fellow who had driven me safely for eight months around the army out-stations of North Malaya. Until a regular driver could be posted, the MTO had supplied a driver from his pool of trainees when required. It was not a tranquillising experience to have a different Indian *trainee* driver for almost every journey.

Take for example: For my weekly visit to a Signals Detachment in the north, my duty-driver reported with my 15-cwt. truck a quarter-of-an-hour late. "Had some trouble starting it, Sahib," the Indian said.

"What trouble?"

"*Ne malum,* Sahib. Don't know, Sir." He threw out his hands in a gesture of resignation, "Very bad engine - *bahut crab wallah.*" Which seemed unbelievable, for the truck was well-maintained and in excellent condition. I saw to that.

A gentle slope led from the bungalow to the hospital-entrance which opened on to a road meeting the main road a quarter of a mile away. This ran through the town. Then by ferry across to the mainland where there were many miles of good, straight Malayan macadam.

Before the vehicle reached the gates, I was comparing him with Natti Singh who would have been through the hospital grounds and along the road to the town in the time it took this one to get through the gears.

"It's all right, Sahib. I'm not used to this *wallah* yet."

"Don't worry," said I.

But when the Indian crawled through the gates in bottom gear; when he found the road making too severe an angle to negotiate in one attempt; and when he went into reverse for a second try, I wondered how soon I myself would have to take over. "I shall be O.K. Sahib." The Indian reassured himself. "It's all right."

There was not much traffic in the town. Once through it and over on the mainland he gained confidence quickly.

My confidence restored itself more slowly. Mile after mile of straight road stripped a piece out of the dense rubber plantations.

Native villages, set in green clearings dotted with coconut trees, relieved the monotony. The Indian's driving improved with the mileage.

Near one village, a bullock-cart lumbered slowly ahead of us. We could see the driver sitting cross-legged between two large earthenware pots. The road here was wide enough to overtake without giving it a thought, but on approaching the cart I saw my driver was cutting it too fine. The dusky brown hand dropped from the steering-wheel to the gear-lever and then back again to clutch the wheel. What he decided to do was merely a half-decision, for he did nothing.

We closed upon the cart and I realised that my driver had no road sense.

I looked out over the truck's side down into the terror-stricken face of the Tamil sitting between his swaying pots, his mouth open wide showing the vivid red splash of chewed betel-nut over tongue and teeth. I glanced quickly from one Indian to the other, from the face of a bewildered bullock-cart driver to the impassioned face of the man at my side peering forward across his steering-wheel.

The near-side front bumper thudded the rim of the cart's broad wheel. Its shafts lifted high in the air as the cart and driver fell over backwards. Curry and rice splashed out of the rocking vessels. The Indian rolled into the road. Relieved of its burden the bullock walked on unsuspectingly. My driver pulled to the roadside some yards ahead of it. The bullock plodded irksomely until it arrived at the rear of the truck. There it waited with inbred patience. We both got out and walked back to the upended cart. Flinging back my hat over my head I stood assessing the damage, thankful that it was not more serious. At most, only a gallon or so of curry and rice was lost.

The two Indians loudly abused each other! They explained, with much hand-wagging and shaking of heads, the lack of virtue in each other's parents and described each other's madness. While all this was going on, I walked over to the bullock, led it back to the cart and implored the men to replace the shafts. I restrained their abuse by offering sincere apologies to the Tamil and a clean ten-dollar note stopped it altogether. 'Some drivers are a menace,' I said to myself as I climbed back into the cab.

"Well, I would like a British driver for a change," I told Pte Tonkins. "Why don't you apply for a posting? You've been a patient in the hospital long enough for your unit not to miss you. And you will soon be A1 again." The young soldier looked up at me, quizzing. "It's two years since I did any driving. Then it was Bren gun-carriers and tanks. Your 15-cwt truck would be tea-drinking in comparison. I would manage that nicely. It's the softest job in the Army."

I watched as he carefully lifted a praying-mantis off a red beret on the locker and held the slender, long-legged insect in the palm of his hand.

Just two days before he was discharged from the hospital, the authority came through for the British soldier, Tonkins, to be put on the ration strength of the Casualty Clearing Station, to be attached as the Padre's driver.

The job he wanted and believed was the softest job in the Army had come his way! I now would be sitting beside a driver wearing the famous red beret of a British Air-borne Division.

We were travelling north again, but got no further than the town.

I felt at first that Tonkins was a bit erratic and driving far too fast but I put it down to lack of practice. Near to the Cinema, a rickshaw-coolie fell over himself to get out of the way.

A Military Police jeep was coming towards us.

Tonkins veered from the centre of the road. He veered too far.

The front wheel leapt over the kerb into the monsoon-ditch. I was thrown forward towards the windscreen but managed to switch off the ignition.

The truck piled up against a concrete pillar of the Cinema entrance.

One comment I had time to make before the crash was: "Be careful, Tonkins! This isn't a ruddy tank!"

The Military Police helped me out.

A gathering crowd of Chinese watched.

Tonkins, unhurt, also stood by watching. His red beret rested at a cocky angle on thick black hair above an ashen face.

'Softest job in the army!' I said to myself.

******

CHAPTER 26

Indian Concerts

I regularly accompanied Major Langford on his rounds in his psychiatric ward and was frequently alongside him when he treated patients. One young Indian soldier, transferred from the Surgical Ward, had a painful, paralysed right arm he was unable to raise, even to shoulder level. They had X-rayed him; the surgeon had examined him thoroughly and found no physical cause for the complaint. It was a psychosomatic problem. Major Langford talked with the boy in Urdu and gained his confidence. He had been six years in the Army; his home was in North India where his father had worked hard for many years on rented land. Since joining the Army he had not been home but wrote and received letters regularly. I watched the psychiatrist test how high the lad could raise the arm, to test his pain threshold. With gentle help, just about to shoulder level! When the Major used the drug P——l and told the boy to raise his arm above his head, he could do so slowly and apparently without pain. Clear of the drug, the paralysis was real; severe and painful.

Eventually, we learned from the lad that his father was heavily in debt to a wealthy landowner who was threatening eviction and prosecution and he was continually writing for his boy to come back home quickly, he needed his help: 'Come home, help me!'

"Padre," said Major Langford, "I remember you as Welfare Officer, once had a chap released on compassionate grounds. Get to know if this chap could be. I think with such a promise we can do something with him."

"How do you mean?"

"We shall see! I think this chap is subconsciously saying to himself, if I can't use my arm I'm useless to the Army, so I will be discharged. Let us work on that assumption and see what happens."

On the psychiatrist's report and testimony, I did eventually get the promise of release.

I was with the Major when he used the drug to implant the message into the boy's subconscious mind. He told him repeatedly; "You can't use your right arm! You are no use to the Army. You would be no use to your father at home. He needs you but you could not help him! You would be useless! When you can use your arm normally, you will be demobbed and free to go home. Raise your arm! Lift it up! Higher!"

Gradually, without the use of the drug, the lad could do that.

In less than three weeks the treatment proved effective. He had full use of the arm and was discharged from hospital, with a release from the Army on compassionate grounds. "An example of the powerful force of the subconscious mind," said the Major. "That is not to say the pain was not real. It was!"

Soon after that incident, I was talking with a 22-year-old patient suffering only a slight touch of malaria. "How long have you been out here," I asked.

"Six months."

"Married?"

"Yes, two years ago to a girl. She's only twenty. It's not right that I should be away from her. I can't tell anybody how I feel - its inside me - I can't do without her - I love her - we were never parted from each other - it isn't right that I should be away - she's young - she goes to bed crying every night - I can't get it out of my mind - I miss her - I must get back to her - it's breaking my heart - I can't stand it any longer."

I sat listening to his moans. "Laddie," I said, "There are many men out here like you and I know how you feel! You want to go home. We all do! I want to go home to a wonderful girl."

"I'll get back by hook or by crook," he interrupted furiously. "I know other fellows are the same but this is different - I must be with her - here's a photo of me six months ago and look at me now."

He continued; "Can you do something for me, sir? I've asked the MO. He has told me he will send me back as soon as I get out of hospital. I've written and told her that I'm going home as soon as I get out of hospital."

I told him; "For you to go home now, the MO would have to say you are medically unfit and in any case, the authorities could stop it. I hope you do get home, but you should not have written to tell her you were going home. It will make things worse for her if you don't get what you want." His moaning went on-and-on.

Finally, I said to him, "You are lucky you know, you are married and will be going home to your wife. I know men whose marriages have broken down while they are out here and even so, they could not get home. When they do, they have no wife to go to. You have!"

Somehow I was sorry for him, but inwardly annoyed. My annoyance arose from remembering the airman who had recently died in the hospital, having been in South East Asia for three years and was actually due to go home; there was a child at home he had never seen!

In readiness for the time when we move to the Civil Hospital we were taking over two nearby bungalows from the RAF. The CO asked me to pack my bags and take them down to one of them before the RAF moves out at 1700 hrs. I told him I had to go to Ipoh and Taiping and had planned to set off at 1500 hrs. I should not be here to do that. I packed all my kit and left it to be taken after I had gone. I was away three days.

It was 2000 hrs. when I arrived back in Penang and I had to find my new quarters. It took an hour to get things sorted. Then back to the hospital for a late dinner.

Together with Capt Ken Brown, the dentist who would be sharing the bungalow, we began to straighten it up. The RAF tykes had left it in a filthy, horrid mess. There were bullet holes in the ceiling from their mad parties!

I had a letter from Billy Sellars who was in India. The lucky lad had been home to England on leave. He told me he had made application for a posting to 'Stars in Battledress' which application had been accepted by the Pool, but turned down by the War Office. He was the young stage-manager in my Tideswell Youth Club productions. (Years later he became a producer with the BBC.)

That night there was an Indian Concert at the hospital and really, it was the finest thing I had seen for a long time. Classical Indian dancing is something I suppose Europeans rarely see. One of the men in an Indian Ballet excerpt was an amazing actor. His expression of emotion was thrilling.

The peak of the evening was the 'Snake-charmer ballet.' The girl who took the part of the snake was superb. Her graceful movements and the expression of her hands were spellbinding. Ken Brown, who is an authority on ballet, said that if they had been in London they would have had five or six 'curtains.' It was most enjoyable.

Rather different from the one I saw before we moved from Ipoh. It was an Indian concert for the Indian troops and as my batman was there, I had to go in the truck to fetch him. At 2230 hrs. the concert was still going strong. (An Indian concert could continue for hours and was not regarded a success unless the audience has been excited to frenzy by weird amazing music and dances.)

There was an example of Indian magic. One of the performers after swallowing a needle-and-thread began to withdraw the thread through the flesh of his stomach.

He walked around for the audience to see that it was no fake. Sitting next to me was one of our doctors who examined the flesh and pulled out some thread; yard after yard of it! Horrid!

At the finale, when all the artists were sitting cross-legged on the stage singing and swinging rhythmically and the audience was clapping in time, a soldier sitting in front of me suddenly lurched out of his seat, fell face downwards on the ground, then began hysterically shouting, jumping and beating himself. While others tried to restrain him, he struggled to get on the stage.

Eventually they overpowered him; but a general fight ensued.

They told me that this frequently happened and I didn't wonder! Had I stayed much longer, the music and noise would have driven me crackers.

******

Chapter 27

"The Jewel Revealed"

On board a troopship, Lieutenant MacDonald's whole personality changed: from being a quiet and reserved lad he developed a flare for social highlight and became the leader of a group entertaining the troops. He was mentally unbalanced and it showed more in the first few days of his landing in Malaya, where he quarrelled with his Commanding Officer about Orders. He was now a patient in the ICCS Psychiatric Ward, a certain schizophrenic, threatening to go to India to see Lord Mountbatten to get that CO fired, together with other senior officers around him. Sitting on the veranda in his usual place, he rose to meet passers-by, assuring them of his sanity. When I came along, he was correcting a typewritten copy of his poem. Gesticulating, he said, "I'm trying to perfect my poem, Padre. It's very difficult to concentrate when a perfectly sane man has been kept in this moon-house for five days." Pointing to the Ward he said, "Do you know George in there?" George was a patient whose sole occupation was to tell all-and-sundry he was God. "George is perfectly sane. I've made him better by talking to him. I know more about psychiatry than the psychiatrist himself does. You believe that, don't you Padre?"

"I must read your poem when it is perfect," I said.

"There's nothing perfect in this world and never has been," he replied. "Jesus Christ wasn't perfect. It says in the bible that Jesus wept. He wept because he was sorry and if a man is sorry for anything he has done, he is not perfect. If he wept, he hadn't self-control of his emotions. Therefore he wasn't perfect."

As Major Crewden-Parkes, our specialist neuro-surgeon, a youngish-looking man was passing, the lad called out, "Major, you'll answer this question for the Padre. There's nothing perfect in the whole world, not even Jesus Christ himself, is there?"

The surgeon, as though in simple faith, argued for Christ's perfection. "There is such a thing as perfection in this world," he replied. Taking my finger in his hand, he said, "Suppose the Padre had a small cyst on his finger, I could cut it away quite simply and it would be a perfect operation."

"But how do you account for Jesus weeping? If he were a perfect man he should have kept perfect self control."

"Jesus wept," said the surgeon in a soft voice "not in penitence but in compassion." He was resting his hands on his thighs behind him, a familiar pose. "I've wept," he said, "and I'm not ashamed of it."

Perhaps because of its unexpectedness, I thought there was something in his last words that offered a rare instance of 'humility in perfection.'

When it was finished, Lieutenant MacDonald gave me a typewritten copy of his poem.

"The Jewel Revealed"
(Composed by a madman in the moon)
Land full of mystery, riches and charm,
Whose scenes fascinate and stories charm,
The temple, the mosque; dhoti and sari
Incense, bazaars; the rickshaw and gari.
Land of romance as believed in the books,
Now I can see how it honestly looks.

Mystery say! What mystery? Where?
Unless how the people just don't seem to care.
The riches are there - gold, silver and stones,
But not for the masses who seem skin and bones.
Only the High Caste, Princes and such
Keep all the wealth that the rest seldom touch.

The charm is unique when you look from afar
At Eastern buildings, domed as they are.
Scenes captivating, and villages quaint
But once you're within the comparisons faint

Unveil the temples, the houses and like,
In villages too, a vast difference you'll strike.
The temple examined is bare and just crude,
The homeliness found in the house far from good.
Worse of the lot are the villagers' plights,
Whose home and environs are pitiful sights,
Bashas, mud-huts, or bricks crudely piled.
Some more advanced with their roofs loosely tiled.
In Summer the heat makes them clammy and hot,
When monsoon descends unprepared they are caught
Thick in the mud then surrounding the place
Damp dripping the homes are a human disgrace.
This on its own makes the visitor blanch,
What crowns the lot is the horrible stench.
What hope is there now for a people like this
With lack of good teaching they all sadly miss.
They wash quite a lot, and are clean in this way,
But rubbish and worse lies, ignored to decay.
Disease haunts the people and children unborn;
Their minds between sense and religion are torn.
The answer's the same when you give it a thought,
They won't know these things until they are taught.
This may be due to a land of this size,
The problem presented you cannot disguise.
If they only considered themselves, 'fellowmen'
Had the thought for another a Scotsman would ken,
Looked at religion and castes in the face
Took out the clauses both senseless and base,
THAT is the way to a probable change
To some high degree, possibilities range.
Good material's there, the brains and the skill

Money's in plenty with no lack of will,
There's hope just in sight if the task they don't shelve
But this land needs help, from each native, himself.

India 1945.

I went to visit George, a young sailor-boy suffering from stresses of war. His bed lay alongside the wall under the large window at the far end of the Ward. For the time being, he believed he was God.

He pointed to the lush greenery and palm-trees outside, which he said proved he was in heaven. However, he was not schizophrenic!

I introduced myself as the Padre.

"You're the Padre?" The boy leaned up on his elbow. "Show me your thumb." He took my outstretched hand, grasped the thumb for a close examination and after careful study, said, "Yes, you're the Padre. You're a hypocrite."

"Ah well," I said. "You should know."

Next morning at breakfast in the Officers' Mess, the Psychiatrist greeted me with a smile. "Padre," he said, "I've a theological problem for you!"

"Go on," I said in excited anticipation. He said,

"During the night, God fell out of bed."

* * * * * *

CHAPTER 28

Bits and Pieces

From my War Diary

11 August. An interesting and important feature of this month is the Muslim feast '*Ramadan.*' From the first sighting of the New Moon, Muslims begin to fast each day from dawn to sunset. At six o'clock every morning, when it is still quite dark with only a suggestion of the dawn, one Indian soldier in our compound, under my window, sings out at the top of his voice a piercing, plaintive wail; a prayer that is used each day at all the Muslim Prayer Temples, bringing to mind a minaret in a desert-town where the priest climbs to sing the Call-to-Prayer and all the faithful kneel towards the East. At first, this singing, a weary sound, annoyed me but I have grown to appreciate this passionate outcry of prayer and devotion, each dawn and sunset. The same singer performs the rite each day. The unique wailing-melody haunts the mind and this will go on until the fall of the Moon.

21 August. We are approaching the rainy season; September to December, when every evening about four o'clock we have rain and storms. It is now ten-thirty, all the windows are open and it is quite warm, the air is balmy after the earlier storms. The only sounds are of barking dogs in the distance and the chirp of many nearby grasshoppers. There is also the funny little croak of the lizards running up and down the walls; friendly little fellows who eat up the flies. I should think they mesmerise the victims, for they remain quite still for a time; the fly does not, or cannot move. Then a sudden dash and a long thrust of the lizard's tongue and the fly is no more.

8 September. Last night Capt Mukerjee, Capt Brown and I went to the 'flicks'. We had dinner at the Boston Café then went along to the Odeon. The film 'Du Barry was a Lady' was silly and it seemed such a waste of 'Glorious Technicolor' to produce such things. However, there is no accounting for people's tastes. Coming home through Georgetown was like walking through Blackpool during the illuminations; brilliantly lighted 'Victory Arches' (erected at a cost of $26,000) looked bright and pleasant. A splendid Arch in Beech Street was built in the traditional Chinese-style, with upsweeping corners and elaborate, colourful decoration.

1 September. Yesterday, we had the party for the farewell of Sister Backhouse. She left yesterday afternoon, as also did one of the BOR's (British Other Ranks). At her invitation, Ken Brown and I went to the Sisters' Mess for tea. Her Indian batman was so affected he was almost in tears. Miss Yang Dahl, the American Methodist Missionary in Penang, rang to invite me to dinner with the Bishop who is in Penang for the weekend and is to preach on Sunday. So I shall have chance to discuss the possibility of coming back to Malaya (presumably married by then) in a year or so. I believe Padre Christian, another Methodist in Singapore also wants to come back.

2 October. Today, Ken Brown's trunk arrived. When he came out to Malaya twelve months ago he was compelled to leave it behind at Liverpool, knowing it would be sent later. It has taken all this time to catch up with him. Most of the contents are in good condition but the lock had been forced open and two tennis rackets stolen, as well as all the clean underclothes and pyjamas; those he had no time in Liverpool to have laundered are still in the trunk. I have not heard yet from Thomas Cook about my trunk, except to receive a receipt for 100 rupees and a note from my bank in Bombay to say the cheque had been cashed. If there is much more delay I shall be home before it reaches me. I hope it arrives safely.

My copy of the New Testament is becoming very much worse-for-wear so this afternoon I took it to pieces page-by-page and interleaved them with sheets of notepaper. I bound it up again and took it to the printers to be finished off in leather-binding. Unfortunately, the printer had no leather in stock so our Quartermaster, Jimmy Blacklaw, came to the rescue and gave me some of the Red Cross supply of leather. I now have a leather-bound interleaved New Testament.

18 October. This morning, the Chaplain General left Taiping to continue his lightning tour of South East Asia Command. He should have arrived at Butterworth airfield, 10 miles away from Penang, last Thursday. Padre Quigley and I were waiting with the Senior Chaplain for five-and-a-half hours for the plane that was to bring him, then we were told it was a day late which meant that yesterday, we all went down to the airfield again. (The SCF told us it was "good discipline to stand and wait.") The signal said he would land at 1215 hrs. However, it was 1440 hrs. when the plane touched down.

We came across to Penang from Butterworth in a special launch, which crossed over in about five minutes instead of the usual twenty-five for the normal ferry. The Chaplain General was quite excited about the visit. He had not been this Far East before. In fact, he is the first Chaplain General to visit these parts officially. We went to the 2nd Battalion West Yorks Regiment (Quigley's Battalion) for tea. There was no time to come across to the ICCS as planned.

At 1700 hrs. the Chaplain General, (CG) the Deputy Assistant Chaplain General (DACG) and the Senior Chaplain to the Forces (SCF) went to the 7th Indian Division HQ in Taiping. Quigley and I went to stay overnight at Taiping for a short conference with the CG this morning, before he continued his tour. He said he had come straight from the War Office to let us know that he is interested in the Brotherhood of Chaplains and he thought it was the best way of showing, what was to him, the greatest fact in life. The friendship of Christ.

He outlined his policy for the future of the Chaplains Department and emphasised his idea of what a Chaplain's job in the Army should be.

It was refreshing to meet him straight from London (a 'pale-skin' in comparison to our browned bodies). All agreed he is an admirable man of first-rate quality for the job.

28 October. Because the 1st Battalion Queen's Royal Regiment in Sungai Patani is without a Padre, I was asked to be attached to them for five weeks.

I expect the posting very soon!

* * * * * *

CHAPTER 29

The Queen's

On November 4th I left 25 ICCS having been 'attached for temporary duty' to the **1st Battalion The Queen's Royal Regt.** on the mainland about 20 miles north of Penang Island. With about 400 British soldiers and 25 officers the unit was waiting in camp at Sungai Patani before moving to Gibraltar in about a month's time. They had recently come from Siam and for a few months have had no Padre. I felt there was good work to be done. The camp was about two miles out of Sungai Patani and the situation was not good. Living quarters were the direct opposite of the CCS hospital's 'luxury.' Give credit, they certainly did their best, giving me a room for myself and an office with a telephone. They had already placed much of the welfare work in my hands.

Next to the Commanding Officer I was the oldest officer; Doc came next; four young subalterns fresh from OCTU joined us. When I arrived, I told the CO that given the opportunity with Padre's Hours, I could get across to every man in the battalion five fundamental truths of practical Christianity, which the Chaplain General suggested should be called 'The Soldiers Religious Manual,' truths about the Christian faith which would improve his life as a soldier and later as a citizen:

(1) Worship – to become a worshipper.
(2) Prayer – to become a pray-er.
(3) Student – to think about one's faith; about one's relationship to God; and to one's environment.
(4) Churchmanship – to become a member of a Christian Community.
(5) Witness – to let people know you are a Christian.

In the first week I conducted ten Padres Hours which meant I had talked with about 300 lads. I was told my stay with the 1st Queens would be five weeks, but then I understood it would be longer. I should have to work out another series.

The Officers Mess was a long 'basha' a wooden structure with a roof of grass-leaves and the whole building, with a veranda running the whole length, was on stilts.

One Sunday afternoon when I was sitting on the veranda outside my room, a few officers were sitting outside their rooms reading. It rained all the afternoon and a heavy thunderstorm brought a lightning-strike very close, because we heard the crash of a splitting tree.

On Sunday morning, November 10, two Companies of the battalion were away; one was on surveillance-duty up in the jungle-foothills; one Rifle Company was moving 42 miles north to Alor Star near to Siam and a large contingent of men was out on an Armistice Day Parade. With so many men away we held my sparsely-attended morning service in the Canteen.

After the Service, I was sitting outside my room and thinking of that first Armistice Day November 11th 1918, when l was a child among others being paraded on a railway-cart; part of the celebrations. The present moment merged into the past with changing scenes and faces - old Mr Turner, the stableman and the runaway horse; the fatal accident of Vera, schoolgirl class-mate; vivacious Lynda Sellars who disappointed me at the Tideswell Sheep-Roast; the holiday at The Lye with Uncle Fred, Aunt Gerty, old Aunt Polly and Floss, the dog; the gold-medallist rose-painter Anthony Connelly; I smiled as I remembered brothers Fred and Joe Soames, old age pensioners; I thought of Esther, my bright and happy sister who taught me to knit and who died so young; The faces of Sister Mary Proctor and Major Maurice Kenneford brought me back to the present.

It rained all that afternoon with a heavy thunderstorm, but it seemed to do little to clear the humid, stifling air.

In the evening, Captain Leslie Milson, the friendly battalion doctor, came along to my room. Doc was a young man with a mass of well-groomed ginger-hair above a wrinkled forehead and a pleasant smile on a round, clean-shaven face. He sat on a bamboo-chair with his long legs resting on the charpoy-bed. For an hour or so, we were discussing religion. The discussion led up to the problem of Evil with the Doctor's remark and question, "We have come through the final stage of a war, which has caused such a total of human misery as must make insignificant the greatest of previous human disasters; the on-going problem, Padre, is this, Why does God allow so much evil in the world?"

I replied, "I agree that War is a gigantic evil, but there is also a vast amount of good."

"If God is all embracing, then evil as well as good must be one of his attributes," said Doc. "In all fairness, how can you postulate an all-embracing God without agreeing that for his own purposes he means evil to exist?"

"What divine purpose can possibly embrace evil?" I asked. I thought of the troopship discussion on the voyage to Malaya and I would have been happy for Capt Mace the agnostic, to be with us now. Doc answered, "God knows well the forces which Man has to struggle against and also the forces with which he has equipped Man to fight them. He cannot in fairness turn and judge or condemn Man over the outcome of a struggle where he himself has balanced the opposing forces. I say again, Evil as much as Good must be one of His attributes."

"That's your assumption," said I. "God has left Man in charge of his own destiny, given him freedom of choice and consequently all humans are responsible before God."

"It *is* my assumption and it seems an inescapable one," replied Milson. "The only purpose one can guess at is that the experience of good and evil is not so much a trial as training of some sort which cannot be derived in any other way."

"I agree," I said. "Perhaps evil and the effects of evil have to be experienced if we are to understand authentic goodness. However, God has given Man free-will and free-choice, choice of evil, choice of good. It seems to me a battle between the two.

A World War 1 Padre said in one of his poems, "I know not why the evil, I know not why the good, I know that both are there, the battle set and I must fight on this side or on that." In that poem his inspiration for the fight was, if I remember rightly,"The light of love, pure love and true, in his mother's eyes." Someone has said "Evil is present only to the extent that love is absent."

"What inspires *you*, Padre?" asked Milson. His blue eyes seemed to crinkle. "I'd like to know!"

"I'll tell you! I believe and have believed for a long time, what Paul said in his great letter to the Romans: 'All things work together for good to those who love God.' The Greek word for 'work together' can also mean 'intermingle.' I prefer that! Good remains good, evil remains evil but they intermingle for good. Nothing changes. The joys and sorrows, the success and failures of life are not obliterated; they intermingle and by God's grace, make something of life that is altogether good and splendid: 'All things intermingle for good to those who love God' is a great message of Hope."

Doc made no comment. "Well, you did ask!" I said. We were silent as we listened to the bugle call 'Lights Out'.

Doc broke the silence. "Is it that man shall not only know good from evil but shall experience both before he can take a fitting part in merging into the higher forms of existence, The Eternal Existence that is God?"

We were content for that to be the last word.

******

6

HONG KONG AND CHINA

CHAPTER 30

Hong Kong

A letter from the **C O 1 QUEENS** dated 23 December, in the usual format of an Army Movement Order, told me -

(1) You have been posted to **HQ Second British Division** and attached to **1 DEVONS.**
(2) You will leave the Bn area in unit-transport and proceed to Kuala Lumpur by road at 1000 hrs. on 29 Dec. You will make your own arrangements as to accommodation whilst in Kualur Lumpur.
(3) You will then proceed to Singapore by Rail.
(4) Full antimalarial precautions will be taken. All drinking water will be chlorinated.
(5) 1 days rations will be taken.
(6) Authy: Chaplains Branch, HQ Malaya Command, letter dated 27 Dec. Part 11 Orders dated 13 March: — Embarked S'pore per MV "DEVONSHIRE" on 21.1.47. Disembarked Hong Kong on 27.1.47.

On the 'DEVONSHIRE' the Officer Commanding Troops was my Commanding Officer at 19 ITC Formby. It was interesting and good to meet him again. The Troopship was very clean and comfortable. With a cabin to myself I was really travelling in luxury, although the sea was rather rough and for a day or two I had a headache. Otherwise, I was quite fit.

There was a good congregation at the Sunday morning service on board.

The voyage took six days and on the Saturday night, although it was still warm, we were ordered to change from tropical-dress to warmer clothing and battledress. We wondered why it was necessary but in the next twelve hours we were in very cold weather and for the first time in nearly two years, I was shivering with cold. In Hong Kong it was comparatively, very cold.

The Devonian Adjutant standing with me on the deck on our approach, said how much the view reminded him of Torquay.

We arrived in Hong Kong on January 26 and disembarked the next day. A military band ('The West Yorks') played for us as the 400 men were loaded into a convoy of 3-ton trucks to proceed to our barracks at Stanley, on the other side of the island.

The hills which rise to rather grim heights, are an outstanding feature of Hong Kong – the town itself is built on the hillside.

Our barracks were high up on a hill 400 feet above sea-level, overlooking the village of Stanley and the surrounding sea. The roads were tortuous and it was our misfortune on the way to Stanley to have a tragic accident. One of the trucks hit a rock and overturned. Three men were killed and 16 injured. Two of the injured died later, one in Queen Mary hospital and the other in 28 IGH. The funeral was a full military funeral. Much of my time since arrival was spent running between the hospital and HQ arranging for the funeral.

A newspaper report read, '*The funeral took place yesterday of the three members of 1st Battalion The Devonshire Regiment who died as a result of a tragic accident last Monday. The burial was carried out with full military honours at the Happy Valley cemetery. Gun carriages of the 27th Field Regt. RA escorted by pall bearers and a firing party from the Devons bore the coffins from the Monument, Gap Road to the Cemetery.*

The burial service was conducted by The Rev G Hatt Lipscomb, (SCF) The Rev A J Ball, and The Rev E Harper (West York's Padre).

Wreaths were laid by representatives of the Army and the RAF Among those present were Col E N Clarke, representing the GOC, Lt Col M C D L Reynolds, and Lt Col H A Borrowdale, CO of the Devon's'

It was my responsibility to lead the cortege and later to send letters to the next-of-kin.

I took photographs of Stanley village and its people. One was published with two others in H B Rattenbury's book '*This is China.*' I was long overdue for leave and took advantage of being in Hong Kong to request authority to visit Lingnan University in Canton. However, before then, I went to Macao on a very cold and rough day. The boat, crowded with about 200 Chinese passengers and four Europeans, sailed at 5.30 p.m. It was 9.00 p.m. when we arrived. Standing on deck, peering through the darkness at the tiny light on the horizon which was Macao, surrounded by Chinese with their baggage, piglets and children, for the first time in the thousands of sea-miles travelled, I felt sick! I felt I could have cheerfully died!

On arrival, a military-truck was waiting to take us to the Leave Centre. 'Us' being myself and a BOR (British Other Rank) who was on duty. The ship's captain told me there was only one Officer in the Leave Hotel, which can accommodate twelve. There was the short journey of 400 yards of Main Street and 200 yards along the waterfront, then Lt Keith Foot who was spending ten days convalescent-leave after an appendix operation welcomed us at the Officers' Centre. After a good meal, I changed into 'civvy' clothes. We had two hours chat and so to bed. Throughout the whole leave the weather was bad. Rain and drizzle almost continually! Nevertheless, that did not prevent sightseeing in the afternoons. I had already visited the British Consul, Mr Hill-Murray, to pay my respects and he invited me, as his guest, to the Rotary Club dinner that night.

Macao is the oldest European colony in the East, having been presented to the Portuguese by the Chinese for help given in clearing the district of bandits. This was about 1557.

The first church built in China was St Paul's, built in 1602. Attached to the church was a famous college, burnt down in1835. The fire spread to the church and destroyed it except for the whole front, which still stands.

A mass of skilfully-worked carvings, done by Japanese Christian artisans, covers the stonework.

It is said that the sight of this ruin inspired Sir John Bowring to compose the hymn 'In the cross of Christ I glory; Towering o'er the wrecks of time.' Near to an old fort, is the graveyard of the old Protestant church built by the East Indian Company in 1821. It was rebuilt in 1922. The first person to be buried in the churchyard was Mary Morrison, the wife of the great pioneer missionary Robert Morrison. She was buried with her unborn child. When Morrison landed in 1807 the Chinese were forbidden under penalty of death to teach a foreigner the language, yet after 27 years he had translated the Old and New testaments and compiled the first Chinese-English dictionary. Another famous person buried in that churchyard was Rt Hon Lord John Spencer Churchill, the 4th son of the Duke of Marlborough. It was a quiet, secluded little spot and one somehow sensed the atmosphere of long ago. Keith Foot told me that the day before my arrival there were some American correspondents 'writing-up' Macao and they had taken scores of photographs of the graveyard and church. There is also the first European hospital in the East, built in 1569 and reconstructed recently. Chinese patients first received treatment at the hands of European doctors and had the first experience of surgery. Another place that interested me was a Chinese temple, where the first treaty between U.S.A. and China was signed in 1844. The stone table specially built for the purpose is still to be seen.

There were eight British residents in Macao, most of whom I met at the Rotary Club dinner. Far the most interesting was the 'Colony King' a Mr Gellian the richest man, rather shrewdly important; owner of the Water-works, and the Electricity. He had an ultra-modern house built on the hill-top called 'Skyline.' His gardens and fountains had a variety of hidden lighting which must have been quite a display when used. He seemed a kind and sober character! The dinner was a many-course Chinese meal. Dr C T Wong was the speaker. In the past, he had been a Chinese ambassador to many countries and, if I heard him correctly, he was at the signing of the Treaty of Versailles but refused to sign because they were handing over Chinese territory to the Japanese. Last night at an anniversary dance at the NAAFI Club for British Service Personnel, I met the governor of the colony and again the British Consul and Mr Gellian.

It had been an attractive two-day's leave and a much fully-occupied one. On the following Sunday, I preached in the Hong Kong Methodist Church. Not a large congregation but it was a pleasant change to conduct a civilian service.

** ** ** **

The official authority for my Canton visit came to the 1st DEVONS from the Colonel in Charge Administration (Col IC Admin.) Land forces, Hong Kong. A copy came to me on 7 March. I was 'granted four days leave' and my visit 'had been arranged by the Consul General Canton.'

I kept a journal of the visit.

******

CHAPTER 31

Hong Kong to Canton

In 1946 I had leave to visit Ling Nan University, Canton and recorded the visit in my journal. I stood on Kowloon railway station waiting for the morning express to Canton. Kowloon is a British possession in the 'New Territories' two miles by ferry from Hong Kong and about 30 miles by rail to the Chinese frontier. The frontier is a seventeen-mile boundary which climbs over the hills and then follows the course of a muddy stream through ripening paddy fields.

Even in the dull light, I wanted to take a photograph but my travelling friends warned me to keep my camera out of sight until we were well away from the Chinese officials. The Chinese were sensitive about some things in their country. They did not like foreigners photographing their beggars, nor their very poor. Officials might have confiscated my camera.

Here-and-there on the platform, people were squatting among their possessions and a queue was waiting to go through the gate for Customs examination. Mothers carried babies slung on their backs inside thick Chinese-quilts; small black heads lolled sideways from the top of the rounded bundles and little wool-clad legs dangled out of the quilt on either side. Grown-up children also had to carry something - parcels or baskets of fresh vegetables. Others, not much more than babes themselves, were carrying smaller children on their hips. Men walked with arms folded, huddling their hands from the chill morning air in the sleeves of their thin jackets. Customs officials, making a hurried search for concealed weapons, checked all Chinese travellers, men and women alike. If there were anything to be found they would find it! It was not unknown for them to catch a Chinese carrying a grenade.

The European police inspector on duty had been interned in Stanley Camp, Hong Kong, where Rev W Ream (Bill) my fellow traveller had spent four dreadful years during the Japanese occupation. Bill was a returned missionary who had lived in China many years. There was a delighted exchange of greetings, then a cursory examination of our passports and documents. Then we were quickly directed through the Customs barrier.

The train was already waiting. We soon organised ourselves in the reserved accommodation in a second-class carriage.

Rev Leonard Hickin, my other fellow traveller, also a returned missionary, was left to guard the luggage while Bill and I walked along the platform to look at the engine, a powerful oil-burning loco, one of UNNRA's gifts to China.

I later watched a consignment of these giants being unloaded in Hong Kong harbour, a special ship-crane picking each locomotive off the boat and carrying it suspended in mid-air like a sack of rice. Our interest in the engine encouraged the Chinese driver to invite us to climb into the cab and there we stood at the controls of this American-built monster, excited as two schoolboys.

The 8.20 through express (No.8) to Canton was ready for the signal 'GO'.

The journey was broken by a frequent procession of officials who were

sometimes accompanied by armed police. Groups of soldiers passed back-and-forth along the train. On one of their trips they brought us a sheet of grubby paper divided into columns, headed with written Chinese characters. Non-Chinese travellers had to give name, age, address, passport-details, purpose of journey, nationality etc. I noticed on the list that Dr J Henry the Principal of Ling Nan University was returning from Hong Kong. Ling Nan University was our destination and I met him there next morning.

An hour's ride through the fresh rolling greenness of the lovely hills and valleys of the leased New Territories brought us close to the frontier. A tented camp and British soldiers wearing the famous green beret of the Commandos warned us that we were very near. We passed a small building flying a British flag at the side of the railway; we were then soon over the steel bridge across the river where groups of Chinese National soldiers in their motley uniforms told us plainly we were in China.

At one stopping-place, an army of hawkers selling Chinese delicacies and tasty dishes besieged the train. Many were children - lovely kiddies! Plates of roast legs of tempting brown chicken sold well and hard-boiled eggs were popular. The more skilful vendors who were able to escape the eyes and boots of patrolling officials did quite a brisk trade. A rampant Inflation had already crippled the country. Some of the morsels cost thousands of dollars. I forget now whether I paid two or three thousand dollars for a hard-boiled egg. We wondered if the unsold dishes were re-cooked for the next train arrival later in the day.

We continued our journey through typical countryside with the cloud-capped mountain range in the distance. Carefully irrigated paddy-fields were set in the hill-basins. Many of the fields were terraced and walled-off by narrow mud-banks. All were lightly covered with water. Water-bullocks high-stepping through the soggy earth were doing the ploughing, the ploughman followed, his trousers rolled high above the knees and his legs plastered with soft, wet soil. Closely-packed beds of growing rice now almost ready for thinning and transplanting into prepared plots showed up evenly as bright patches of green. This was already being done in some fields. The plants were set in perfect rank-and-file at about a foot-or-so from each other. The coolies, standing knee-deep in water, took advantage of the passing train to straighten up and rest for a few minutes, holding their begrimed hands outstretched away from their clothes.

We caught glimpses of small villages, compact and colourless. Drab houses mostly built of sun-baked mud bricks. However the roofs, graceful with their upward curves of carved wood and dull-green glazed tiles of scalloped design, compensated for the drabness of the walls.

The journey took four and a half hours and we reached Canton by lunchtime.

Within a few moments of our stopping at Canton station (Kwong Chow East), even while we were reaching for our luggage from the rack, Chinese railway-workers had scurried along the coaches cleaning the train and whipping away the morning newspapers from the tables.

They not only cleared the newspapers but took the half dozen books we had brought with us. "Keep an eye on your luggage and watch your pockets!" said my friend. A bright young high-school Chinese girl sitting opposite had already warned us. She had only slender knowledge of the English language. One of her perfectly well-spoken English sentences would end a conversation – "I don't understand, please tell me in Chinese." However, she did tell me to take care! "Many pickpockets here!" I asked Bill, who had a better command of Cantonese, to tell her that somebody had already pinched my pipe. She chuckled too heartily when he had finished. Leonard, the linguist of our party, said he had given the wrong intonation for the word 'pipe' and had told her that pickpockets had already stolen my 'chimney.'

In clearing the station, all the passengers queue up in two single files which crocodile to either end of the platform and return to the centre exit. There were enough police and soldiers to make sure no one broke the queue and they were not over-modest in booting some offenders. Estimating that it would take almost fifteen minutes for the station to clear, we stood at the door and waited. There was no preferential treatment!

Once outside the station we began a discreet bargaining with the rickshaw coolies for conveyance to the YMCA, a temporary stopping place on our way to Ling Nan University.

After some time we were in procession with a long line of rickshaws meandering at a quick trot-pace towards the city. My first impression of Canton was of a desert town. The traffic and running coolies kicked up thick clouds of reddish dust, like sand-clouds and in this red blanket we frequently lost sight of the bumping rickshaws. The roads were in an atrocious state. It was a miracle that a new 'bus lasted as long as three months on these so-called Canton roads. We were told that the city was too poor to keep them in repair. That may be true, or perhaps kinder to say that materials were not available; a better explanation at any rate for the sake of gallant China!

'Canton was a thriving port long before the Christian era and Arabs were bringing merchandise here eight hundred years after the death of Christ. But it was not until the sixteenth century that the sea route to China was re-discovered and the West made further impact upon the East. The city then became an important link and remained so for many years.' I understand that although Canton has its roots in history there is no building more than 200 years old. The oldest parts with their narrow, unsanitary streets were filthy, yet in the most unlikely places one found treasures of art and craftsmanship. However, there are some delightful places, restful and quiet. Shameen is one such. Isolated by a canal, it was a non-Chinese settlement until recent years. Many of the houses are large two-storied buildings in Italian style, with lawns and gardens shaded by tall trees. A hundred years ago it was an unreclaimed flat on the riverbank.

The river itself with its ferries, sampans, junks and houseboats is a hive of activity. Hundreds of Chinese live in these boats. The strange destiny of children born in this town-on-water is to spend their lives entirely on the river and to possess no other home. This is especially true of the girls and the adult women-folk who look after the boats while the men work on the land and return to their boat-dwellings at night.

Our rickshaws brought us to the YMCA and I was surprised to find such a flourishing branch. During lunch, the American manager came trundling along on his heavy USA pushbike. He told us that in the broadest sense there was a membership of 2,000.

All who contributed to the funds regarded themselves as members, but active membership was about 200. Young Chinese take a keen interest in the Scout organisation and Youth Club activities.

Lunch finished, we set out in a jeep for the Memorial Gardens, a green seclusion in the heart of the city. It needed a jeep to stand up to the broken surfaces of these Canton roads. From the Gardens, we went to the Sun Yat Sen Plynth and Museum. National Soldiers used the ground floor of the Museum as a barracks but in the upper floors were valuable works of art and antique treasures - priceless pottery and relics of ancient dynasties. From the Museum top-floor veranda we could see the city lying drab below. In the haze of the dull afternoon distances seemed immeasurable. White Cloud Mountain in the distance beyond the river seemed to stand on a line of silver ribbon, torn in one place by Honam Island. Such a view of the mountain is the motif for the design of Ling Nan University badge. The many temples and pagodas breaking the skyline made an ethereal contrast with the tall chimneys of a cement works away to the north.

When the Japanese began their occupation the Chinese adopted a Scorched-earth policy hoping to destroy the whole of Canton but the attempt was a failure. Large devastated areas of the city were still a pitiable memorial.

Our next visit was to the Sun Yat Sen Memorial Hall, said to be among the most beautiful buildings in the world. Dr Sun Yat Sen was one of the first graduates from the Hong Kong Medical School. He is reputed to have called Hong Kong 'The Lighthouse' and wrote in a famous passage, 'I begin to wonder how it was that Englishmen could do such things with a barren rock within seventy or eighty years, while in 4,000 years China has no place like Hong Kong.' Every Monday morning in the circular central hall, an impressive auditorium, his will is read out to the hundreds of Chinese students who attend this weekly memorial service.

On our way back to the YMCA we called at one or two of the many temples. One was a Mecca of successful university students who come to give thanks to Buddha. We were shown thousands of wooden-blocks covered with minute and carefully-carved characters and pictures, rich book-treasures representing centuries of skilful labour and learning. They were somebody's headache, because unfortunately they seemed to be useless; nobody knew what to do with them. In this temple as in others, there were lavishly-adorned shrines and fine elaborate wood-carvings.

After coffee and biscuits at the YMCA, we caught a 'bus to Ling Nan and once inside the university we felt to be in a different world. The hospitality was most generous and we spent a delightful evening in the university campus. Before supper, we saw the model village built in the grounds. Chinese agriculture has become a subject for modern scientific study and full information about Chinese life is now available on the doorstep of Ling Nan.

The model farm was a delightful, gratifying sight. The agricultural side of the University had a Dairy farm and a good herd of cows, a piggery and stables. Crops and rice by the acre provide facility for experiment.

The next day we were conducted through the university itself - through its lecture rooms, its laboratories, its dining halls, its recreation room, its milk-bar (with cream from its own farm), its wonderful library and its playing fields.

The university buildings are truly typical Chinese-style architecture with curved swooping roofs and colourful corners. The grounds are beautifully-kept parkland.

How long it will be before rural China becomes anywhere near the like of that model village only the gods know, but here at least was an inspired dream coming true.

There were over 800 resident pupils, young Chinese from many parts of that vast country; only a few of them were directly concerned with the science of agriculture, but all must have gone back to their homes with an assurance of what might be achieved in their country.

Ling Nan University is a remarkable centre of culture and learning, founded on faith.

However, it has not been free from struggles in a war-crippled country.

Because of inflated currency and the changing scale of human values, a university professor had received, at times, less than a girl clerk in a Canton city office.

Ling Nan was a symbol of faith and certainly no mean achievement.

And I know that all over the world 'faith in right values can result only

in achievements towards right ends.'

******

Chapter 32

Canton to Fatshan

I had travelled from Hong Kong to Canton with two ministerial colleagues, Rev William (Bill) Ream and Rev Leonard Hickin, returned missionaries who had spent many years in China. They were going a further ten miles to Fatshan, to the Methodist hospital, school and orphanage. I decided to go with them.

I wrote in my journal: - No passport! No Visa! My only document of authority was the one from Colonel IC Adm, Land Forces, Hong Kong granting leave to proceed from Hong Kong to Canton. With verbal permission from the Consul General Canton for the next journey to Fatshan, I felt assured that all would be easy. How nearly true that proved to be! I had my fears at the start. Leonard had a British passport and a Chinese visa, a most official-looking document covered with neat red Chinese characters and bearing two 'chop' marks with signatures. Bill had an emergency passport in addition to a visa. I had nothing at all like it, but hoped for the best and trusted to Bill's unpredictable knowledge of Cantonese. Here I was in Canton, without the slightest trouble from the authorities but there were ten miles further to go.

As soon as we came to the station-barrier where Chinese police were standing with rifles over their shoulders, my heart sank! They were asking for passports. Bill produced his! So did Leonard! I fumbled in my battledress pocket, produced an Army Book 439 (a book of personal records) and opened it at random. 'Courses Attended' headed the page. The entry 'Intake Course Tidworth' had the RAChD Reception and Depot Centre's official stamp with the signature of a Senior Chaplain.

I put the open book into the hands of the Chinese police-officer. He very carefully scrutinised it, taking his time while I waited anxiously. At last, he returned it to me with a perfectly lovely smile, a delightful Chinese bow and a distinctly American "That's OK." It was obvious he could neither read nor speak English. I picked up my bag and cleared-off after the others towards the train, thankful that together, Chinese official and I had 'saved face'.

The train was notorious! Leonard with his usual pessimism had warned us we would be lucky if it were running at all. He said it failed to make the journey these last three mornings. In these days of scarcity the ten-mile journey would take anything from one to three hours. No coal to feed the boiler! Only logs collected fortuitously! Much also depended upon the temperature of the day; if the weather were cold it would need a miraculous amount of human energy to keep up enough steam pressure for the wheels to turn. It was like that!

The four nearest coaches were fairly filled with passengers. Women with rattan-baskets holding squealing pigs were still clambering inside coaches, shaped like cattle-trucks and without seats. We walked further along and climbed into a second-class carriage by means of a vertical iron-rung ladder. The steps I felt would cause trouble. They did! The train was drawing to a standstill at one of the country stations, a small wooden building set in the heart of paddy fields, when I noticed some Chinese civilians escorted along the platform by armed soldiers. The prisoners had heavy chains around their necks, arms tied behind them with ropes, chained to each other. They were making their way in single file towards the front carriage. The train drew to a standstill. I grabbed my camera, rushed to the door and started to climb down. After the first rung, the others were unnecessary because in stumbling, I fell, full length on the ground, my camera hurtling away in the air.

It proved an amusing incident for a group of Chinese coolies standing nearby. They chuckled heartily and made their delight quite clear for me and for everyone else to see. By the time I had recovered the camera and myself, the prisoners were climbing into the train. I did the same and nursed my shock for the next ten minutes.

The journey took just over an hour. When we alighted at Fatshan it took another quarter-hour to walk into the town following the procession of passengers. The prisoners and escort were also in the procession. Reaching the main road they apparently grew tired of the journey, or disliked the publicity, for they tried to stop an approaching bus by standing in the centre of the road. The bus side-tracked them. The idea was infectious. The soldiers commandeered the next bus that came along and with some difficulty put the prisoners aboard.

In Fatshan Main Street prayer-pillars stood at intervals where, we were told, orphan children mostly girls were sometimes left to die. Passing the shops, we came to the starting-point for trips up-and-down the river. We hired one of the house-boats to take us to the hospital. The Chinese who managed these boats were distinctly higher-class ladies. The boat was delightfully clean with a bright colourful cabin, its arched roof and wall-panels gaily painted in bright enamel colours. A mirror was built into a small cupboard and rush-mats on a floor of highly-polished loose boards served as beds for the occupants. In the stern were cooking-utensils and over a charcoal fire, a pot containing what seemed to be breakfast porridge.

The ladies removed two of the planks and we sat on the floor with our feet in the boat's nether regions. They took up their rowing positions. Using one oar each, they brought their weight forward on the oars in a rhythmic swing and then the weight of the body took them sliding back along the wooden floor. Their bare feet sliding to-and-fro had given a high polish to the surface and had scooped out identical hollows on each side of the boat.

Soon we were at the gate of the hospital compound. Leonard assured us that this better class houseboat-owner expected a recognised courtesy on being paid. The 2,000 dollars national Currency which the journey cost must not be handed to them as though they were coolies but left discreetly on the seats we had occupied.

We stepped from the boat into the hospital grounds. A few minutes walk brought us to the doctor's house, to the refreshment of a wash and change of clothes for the day had developed hot and sultry.

There were 580 scholars in the Middle School. The Senior Middle was divided into Arts and Science classes. Students ran Night School for the street-children. There were English bible-classes and evening prayers. We took photographs of the thirty or more young children in the orphanage attached to the hospital and a photograph of the ceremony at sundown, - the lowering of the flag by a smart company of young cadets. One special photograph was of the child who escaped from Canton when her parents were killed in the fighting. We heard a very moving story. Although badly crippled she had struggled at a very tender age to walk ten miles to Fatshan and eventually found herself in the safety of the Orphanage.

I stayed there two days and told myself that if nothing more, the visit to the Orphanage, meeting that brave child and hearing her story would alone have made the journey worthwhile. The special photograph was of a brave, smiling, happy child!

Her name was 'May See.'

* * * * * *

CHAPTER 33

Two Choices

When due for demobilisation I faced two choices.

Bishop Amstutz asked me to transfer to the Church in America.

The DACG (Deputy Assistant Chaplain General) wanted me to remain in the Regular Army as Senior Chaplain to the whole of Burma Command.

I rejected both offers!

I intended to go home to marry a wonderful girl who was waiting for me, Dorothy Hall, Dr L Du Garde Peach's actress protégé 'of star quality' his 'attractive little minx of a Cleopatra.'

I sailed back home to the UK on the '*ALCANTARA*' in May 1947 and thereby missed a most severe English Winter. In North Derbyshire snow had drifted to the bedroom window of 'Ivy Cottage' and to get out from the door they had to dig a tunnel. However, it was a glorious summer.

On August 16 1947, Dorothy Hall and I were married in The Fountain Square Methodist Church, Tideswell, North Derbyshire - the Church in which I had made a botch of my first wedding service.

The Revd J Baines Atkinson and Sister Molly Tyson officiated.

******

THE END

Rev A J Ball, HCF
12 The Glen
Sheffield
S10 3fN

Appendix

This was published in the *BOLTON EVENING NEWS*
2nd February 1957

SHORT STORY

The Rake-off

By ALBERT *BALL*

The Regimental Quartermaster's knife was in the Battalion Doctor. The feud had gone on for months.

Dr. Ian MacPherson had been born with a potentially prominent nose and the ability to say what he thought. Known in the battalion as the 'red-headed drain stinker,' he was popular with all ranks, except the Quartermaster.

The dislike had arisen because the Doc had confronted 'Q' with the rumour that he was receiving a large rake-off from the wealthy Indian contractor who supplied the camp with goods.

The feud goes on.

Take last Sunday for example.

Lunch in the Officers' Mess consisted of sliced spam, chips and tinned tomatoes, followed by bananas.

"What an Army," said Doc picking up the menu – a recent idea to place a written one on the table each day. "Sweet . . . fresh fruit. Day after day what?" He twisted his wry mouth as he spoke. "Day after day it says fresh fruit. Fresh fruit indeed, is it? Bananas! Look at 'm."

The silence was broken by the young M.T. officer, a newcomer to the battalion.

"Doc, what's that disease in children that bananas are good for?" he asked.

"Sprue." Doctor MacPherson rippled his tongue around the word.

"What is Sprue, Doc?" asked the boy.

"Fatty diarrhoea," was the reply.

The Quartermaster glowered across the table.

"Sunday lunchtime talk again Doctor?" he said. "Pass a banana!"

The Doc wrinkled the lines of his broad forehead into an odd pattern as he offered the plate in front of him.

"Do they sell 'em by the pound, Quartermaster? Look at this lump of tree here. Is this the contractor's rake-off to the 'Q' staff?"

"Don't talk shop in the Mess" he replied.

So rapping was his voice that it seemed to the young officer that a round of ammo had been fired across the table.

The latest skirmish between the two of them arose from 'Q"s job as Temporary Acting Security Officer. During this transit period the C.O had enforced strict discipline and punishments were heavy.

The battalion was awaiting embarkation orders. Security measures were clamped down rigidly. Every out-going letter was censored, a task shared by all officers.

The Doctor read his daily bundle between sick parade and morning rounds.

He ambled from the M.I. room on Monday morning, across the parade ground where four 'jankers' men were doing pack-drill in the hot sun.

In his bungalow he sat down to the pile of letters on the table. He read, rubber stamped and initialled them in an impersonal way. They were afterwards collected unsealed, by an orderly corporal who took them to the Quartermaster's office where they were prepared for mailing and where sometimes 'Q'would check over a few letters chosen at random.

Doc was reading Private Tompkin's letter to his mother. Suddenly he flicked his right ear, a trick he had. Hooking the forefinger of his left hand over the bridge of his nose he read the letter again:

> 'Dear Mum,
>
> 'Don't worry, but life's getting unbearable. We can't call our souls our own. I'm sick of the battalion. Hope you don't mind me grumbling, Ma, but we've got to tell our bloomin troubles to someone. Our C.O. is a ruddy tyrant. He wants a bomb putting under his bed. We had a parade on Friday - a pukka one. Brigadier's inspection, they call it. You know Tom Jenkins, my pal I told you about. Well, next morning he was up on C.O.'s orders. He was told he wanted a haircut and was given 14 days detention with pack drill. Just for a haircut. It's not ruddy fair. The Brigadier himself was like Lloyd George. He hadn't had a hair cut since he joined the Army. Poor Tom's doing detention now...'

The Doc sat quietly indecisive. Then he turned the air-mail letter over, inked the rubber stamp and pressed it firmly on the top right hand corner, initialled the appropriate line and placed the letter on the growing pile. He finished reading the others and left them in a tidy heap for the orderly to collect

* * *

Next day, the Colonel sent his compliments to the Doctor and asked would he kindly report at his office at 09-30 hours.

He was not in a pleasant mood when the Doc stood before him. On the desk lay Private Tomkin's letter to his mother.

"Doc, I have more confidence in you as my M.O. than as a battalion censor," rasped the C.O.

"I hope so, sir," was the reply.

"You must have a fine sense of what is worthy to morale to give a ropey letter like this the O.K."

"I respect that judgment coming from you," said the Doc.

"That's surprising, since you approve Tomkin's sentiments to his mother."

"I admit, sir," said the Doc, "it caused me some concern, but I felt it was a private expression of personal opinion concerning the treatment of one of his friends."

"It was your job to censor the expression of that opinion. Discipline, Doctor!

Morale, Doctor! For the sake of morale and discipline you should have cut it out."

"I understand sir that the present censorship is mainly for reason of security. There was no incitement in the letter and the information that the Brigadier needed a hair-cut is of little interest to the Japs."

"But what the man says about his commanding officer is of vital interest to me and to the battalion," bellowed the C.O.

"I agree that..." began the Doc.

"And in future a man will not be allowed to write his perfidious opinions of the unit or his officers to his dear mother."

"Sir, I have to tell you respectfully that last night I wrote to my mother, who has a nice sense of humour and I told her all about it. I censored the letter myself"

The C.O. bristled.

"I also told her," continued the Doc, "that not only did the Brigadier need a hair-cut but that I did, too and the Colonel."

Both seemed to be regarding each other silently for a time.

Then, the Doctor's right ear twitched noticeably.

The C.O. saw it. His eyes twinkled involuntarily and he laughed out loud.

"Orderly!" he shouted.

The soldier appeared in the doorway and saluted smartly.

"Take this letter to the Quartermaster with my compliments and tell him to see that the Post Corporal gets it in the afternoon's mail."

He dismissed the orderly.

"Doctor," he said. "You will report at the Camp Barber's today at 17-00 hours. We'll each have a hair-cut."

* * *

Last night in the Mess, the shorn Doctor greeted the Quartermaster with:

"Well, the Regimental Quartermaster doesn't seem to get much rake-off from his job as Security Officer."

"You go and give yourself a blue-pencil injection before censoring any more letters," was the reply.

And so the feud went on.

* * * *

Audrey Bogie
56 The Mount
Selby
NY YO8 9BD

This book was
given to me
by the Rev A. J. Ball
2012.
when he was 99yrs old.

Lightning Source UK Ltd.
Milton Keynes UK
UKOW052155180412

191004UK00001B/17/P

9 781781 480182